From Your Friends At **The MAILBOX®**

Back-To-School Book

GRADES 1–3

Editor In Chief:
Marge Michel

D1309343

Product Director:
Kathy Wolf

Editors:
Cynthia Holcomb, Sharon Murphy

Copy Editors:
Lynn Bemer Coble, Laurel Robinson,
Jennifer Rudisill, Debbie Shoffner, Gina Sutphin

Artists:
Jennifer T. Bennett, Cathy Spangler Bruce,
Clevell Harris, Barry Slate, Donna K. Teal

Typographers:
Scott Lyons, Lynette Maxwell

Cover Artist:
Jennifer T. Bennett

www.themailbox.com

©1997 by THE EDUCATION CENTER, INC.
All rights reserved.
ISBN# 1-56234-162-6

Manufactured in the United States
10 9 8 7 6

Back-To-School Book
From Your Friends At *The Mailbox*®
Grades 1–3

About This Book

Look between these covers to find everything you need to make your back-to-school experience a success! We've included all-new ideas to help you get ready for the first day, organize your materials, set up your classroom, and create eye-catching bulletin boards. We've selected teacher-tested tips on getting acquainted with students, managing your class, establishing routines, making home-school connections, and much more. The ideas and activities in this book are arranged so that you can refer to a topic quickly, then choose the ideas suited to your individual needs. All the topics and ideas are designed specifically for the primary classroom. We hope our *Back-To-School Book* helps you get your school year off to a great start!

Table Of Contents

Getting Ready

Coming Attractions

This welcome-back idea is just the ticket to help students anticipate the first day of school. A week before the big day, mail each of your new students a special admission ticket to your class. Enclose a list of "Coming Attractions"—a sneak preview of projects, themes, and events that will take place in the first weeks of school. (See the patterns on page 73.) Students will be comforted to know what to expect in their new classroom, and parents will appreciate the information about your curriculum plans.

Betty Silkunas—Gr. 1
Oak Lane Day School
Blue Bell, PA

ADMIT ONE
Great Student Into
The Classroom

signed _____ Mrs. Weitzel _____

WELCOME!

Photo Fun

Be prepared for all the many photographs you will take during the school year by purchasing a photo album during the summer. Start off by taking a picture of each student on the first day. Pictures of assemblies, field trips, and class parties will soon follow, and your album will be on hand to hold the prints. Place the album in your class library for students to enjoy. At the end of the year, give each student a few photos to take home. You'll pass on many happy memories of the school year.

Kelly Wong—Gr. 2, Berlyn School, Ontario, CA

A Very Rewarding Idea

Be on the lookout over the summer for promotional items that can help stock your reward box. You'll find that pencils, key rings, and stickers are often given away during advertising campaigns. Health fairs, grand openings, and fast-food establishments often carry items that work well as student prizes, and are usually eager to donate to a school-related cause. As you enjoy the summer months, you'll be surprised at the items you collect for your special students.

VaReane Heese
Springfield Elementary, Omaha, NE

Plan-Book Preparations

As you set up your lesson-plan book for the year, much of the same information has to be recopied from week to week. Music class, lunchtime, recess duty, and spelling tests are standard entries in the schedule, but have to be noted on each week's plans. Simplify your planning time by creating a master list that can be clipped to your plan book each week. Include classes and activities that remain constant from week to week, providing a blank to fill in a page number if necessary. Your planning time will be greatly reduced, leaving you free to take care of the many other tasks that are always at hand.

Vicki O'Neal—Gr. 2, Lincoln School, Baxter Springs, KS

Lesson plans for the week of _____
Vicki O'Neal   2

Subject:	Reading	Every Day Counts	Spelling	Duties Special Classes
Monday	Daily Assignment notes are in reading notebook.		Calendar Activities	Introduce new unit-write 5x or take test	Music Days Music: 1:00 Library: 1:25 P.E. Day 1:00
Tuesday				Peer-tutoring	Lunch duty
Wednesday				Trial test Prac. sheet	Morning recess Guidance 8:30-8:55
Thursday				Practice sheet	Afternoon Recess
Friday				Mastery Test	Alternate morning recess

Spelling Cast-A-Spell
three ring binder, bottom right desk drawer

Math
workbooks in students' desks

Language
Handwriting/Composition

Health Book: Choosing Your Health

Social Studies
Book: Neighborhoods

Specials
Recess 10:15

Duties/Reminders
* Materials in red bins, tallest file

Simplifying For A Substitute

Be prepared for a spur-of-the-moment substitute with a list of important classroom details. Copy a blank page of your lesson-plan book and fill in important information under each subject heading. Make notes telling which textbooks are stored in students' desks, and which are kept on a bookshelf. Indicate where handwriting paper can be found, and where each teacher's manual is kept. Include information regarding students who need to leave the room at certain times of the day. When the necessary details have been filled in, laminate the pages and paperclip them to the current week of your lesson-plan book. If an unexpected need for a substitute teacher arises, you'll rest assured that all the details are taken care of.

adapted from an idea by Mary Dinneen—Gr. 2
Mountain View School
Bristol, CT

Super Binder

Stay organized all year long with a binder that keeps track of all your important papers. At the beginning of the year, purchase a large three-ring binder and a package of pocket-type section dividers. Anticipate the sections you will need to refer to during the year, such as parent correspondence, faculty memos, schedules, and classroom volunteers. Label a divider for each section and file them alphabetically in the binder. As pertinent information comes across your desk, file it in the divider pocket or use a holepuncher to fit the paper in the binder rings behind the appropriate section. Not only will you be more organized, you will also have an ongoing record of the school year.

Susan Wilson—Gr. 1, Sevierville Elementary School, Sevierville, TN

Say, "Cheese!"

As you prepare materials for the first day of school, make sure to have a camera on hand. A photograph of each student can be used in a number of creative ways:
- Display a photograph of the daily leader.
- Place the photographs in a decorated basket. When you need a helper, select a student by reaching into the basket and randomly choosing a photo.
- Group photographs together to show students which cooperative group they will work with.
- Photocopy the original photographs and use on nametags, coat hooks, newsletters, bulletin-board displays, and birthday graphs.
- Display student photos on a poster titled "Look Who's Lost A Tooth!"

Sarah Mertz, Owenton, KY

Tracking The Teacher

To set the stage for a first-day discussion, pick up a few postcards during the summer to send to your students-to-be. Ask to receive a copy of your new class list as soon as it is ready. Collect a supply of postcards from various locations and mail one to each student on the list. Write a brief message of introduction, and explain that you are looking forward to having the student in your class. Ask the student to bring the postcard to class on the first day of school. Students can compare the postmark of each postcard, then discuss their own summer adventures. Your cheerful postcards will initiate a first-day discussion of travel tales!

Vicki O'Neal—Gr. 2, Lincoln School
Baxter Springs, KS

Oh, Goody!

Treat your students to an exciting new year with these back-to-school goody bags. Fill clear plastic bags with items such as pencils, erasers, stickers, and small snacks. Tie each bag with a ribbon and place one bag on each desk. As students come in on the first day, allow them to explore their bags. Students will know right away that being in your class is a real treat!

Nicole Iacovazzi—Gr. 3
Owego Elementary School
Vestal, NY

Skill Baskets

Purchase a supply of small plastic baskets during the summer and fill them with skill reinforcers to use in your classroom. Determine which skills you want students to work on at the beginning of the year, and make sets of cards to help reinforce each skill. Sets of color words, ordinal numbers, shapes, and sight words can easily be written on index cards and stored on large metal rings. Store the completed sets of cards in the baskets. Place a basket of cards in the center of each group of desks. When you need a five-minute filler or an activity to occupy those who complete their assignments quickly, direct students to review a set of cards from the basket. Add new card sets as vocabulary, math facts, and sight words are introduced. With this variety of skills on hand, you can make every minute count.

Linda Parris—Gr. 1,
West Hills Elementary School, Knoxville, TN

Low-Cost Lap Desks

If you use lap desks in your classroom, make note of this thrifty tip! Low-cost and no-cost desks can be acquired by asking for materials from local eating establishments. Cafeteria trays and cardboard pizza boxes make wonderful lap desks and can be purchased for a nominal amount, and are often given to teachers free of charge. If desired, cover the trays and boxes in decorative Con-Tact® paper. The desks come in handy when students sit on the floor for group activities, put puzzles together, or need extra room for art projects. You'll find dozens of uses for these desks, and appreciate how easy they are to store when not in use.

Nancy Bauer—Gr. 2, Kidwell Elementary, Iowa Park, TX

Get-Ahead Graph

Before the new school year is under way, prepare for a year-round graphing activity by constructing this reprogrammable diagram. Design a bar graph with several columns on a sheet of poster board. Title the graph "What Did You Wear To School Today?" Leave an open area under each column so the topic of the graph can be changed each day. A picture of a long-sleeve shirt and of a short-sleeve shirt can be featured one day; the next day it can be changed to show a slip-on shoe and a lace-up shoe. Each student charts his response by writing his name on a self-stick note and attaching it to the correct column. It will take only a few minutes of your day to reinforce graphing skills, and students will enjoy contributing the data.

Kathleen Geddes Darby—Gr. 1
Community School, Cumberland, RI

Park It Here!

Bring a touch of the outdoors into your classroom with this attractive and practical reading area. Purchase two wooden park benches and arrange them in a corner of your classroom. Place a silk tree between the benches, or mount a tree cutout on the wall behind the area. Students will enjoy visiting the peaceful setting for independent reading time, and the benches can also be used for group lessons, or as seating when visitors come to the classroom. The arrangement is not only aesthetically pleasing, but convenient too!

Nancy Bauer—Gr. 2
Kidwell Elementary, Iowa Park, TX

Cozy Classroom

Create a comfortable and cozy atmosphere in your classroom by adding a few pillows to the decor. Accenturate a back-to-school theme with a cushion in a bright apple print for the teacher's chair. Matching pillows in your reading center will highlight the arrangement. The cushions can be changed to emphasize a unit of study, such as the ocean or the rain forest. Find a fabric pattern to coordinate with the desired look for your classroom, and dress up the area with comfort and style.

Kathleen Geddes Darby—Gr. 1
Community School, Cumberland, RI

Quiet Quarters

With minimal effort, you can transform an old card table and a bedsheet into a private reading area for students to use during independent reading time. Provide an assortment of markers and a solid-color flat sheet for students to illustrate with scenes from their favorite books. Drape the decorated sheet over the card table, pinning back two corners to create an entryway. Post a weekly sign-up sheet by the table to allow everyone a special time to be alone with a good book.

Rosemary Linden
Royal Valley Elementary, Hoyt, KS

End With The Beginning

Beat the back-to-school bulletin-board blues with a head start in June. As you're taking down the last bulletin board of the school year, make a little extra effort and put up your "Welcome Back" display. Cover the new board with the background paper from the previous display to protect it over the summer months. What a wonderful feeling it will be to come back in August and know that your bulletin board is ready to greet a new group of students!

Vicki O'Neal
Lincoln School
Baxter Springs, KS

Co-Worker Kit

What could be more encouraging for a new co-worker than this Welcome Kit on her desk on the first day of school? During the summer, collect the items listed below. Place them in a supply box or gift bag with a note explaining the significance of each item. Your thoughtfulness will be the perfect solution to first-day jitters!

- a rubber band, to remind us to be flexible

- a toothpick, to help us pick out the good in every situation

- a stick of gum, to remind us to stick together at all times

- an eraser, to remind us that everyone makes mistakes

- a Hershey's® Hug, to remind us that everyone needs a hug now and then

- a balloon, to encourage us to soar to new heights

- Lifesavers® candy, to remind us that we can depend on each other at all times

- a maze, to remind us to create amazing learning experiences for our students

Sandra Kuhn—Principal, Laveen School, Laveen, AZ

Organizing Materials

Storage Hang-Ups

Reduce closet clutter with this tip for storing small items. Purchase a tiered skirt hanger and a supply of gallon-size zippered plastic bags. Place math manipulatives, craft items, and other hard-to-store items in each bag. Attach each bag to a clip on the hanger, and your supplies are organized. Not only is the hanger a space saver, but the bags allow you to see the items so you can quickly locate supplies.

Rosemary Linden, Royal Valley Elementary, Hoyt, KS

Manipulative Storage

Looking for a way to store math manipulatives that are needed frequently but become lost when stored in the students' overcrowded desks? Try hanging a supply bag on the back of each student's chair. Banks are often willing to donate canvas bags with ties sewn onto each end—perfect for tying to chair rungs! Manipulatives can be placed in the bags until needed, eliminating the need to distribute and collect materials each time an activity calls for manipulatives. Students will have ready access to the necessary supplies without losing a minute of instructional time.

Nancy Bauer—Gr. 2, Kidwell Elementary, Iowa Park, TX

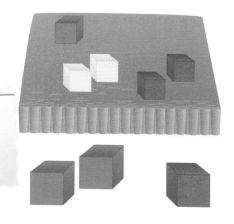

Carpeted Desktops

Many classrooms have a supply of carpet squares on hand to use when activities call for students to sit on the floor. Have you ever thought of using those same carpet squares to cover a desktop? Distribute a square to each student the next time pattern blocks or manipulatives are being used. The carpeted surface will help stabilize the materials, but better yet, it will muffle the sound of the objects being manipulated. How nice to get more mileage from materials already on hand!

Nancy Bauer—Gr. 2, Kidwell Elementary, Iowa Park, TX

Recess Treasures

As you organize materials through-out the year, you're sure to come across supplies that you have had on hand for several years but have not put to good use. As a teacher, you know it's too hard to simply throw them out. Make these supplies available for your students to peruse by labeling them "OK For Recess." Students know they may have access to the materials for art projects, game ideas, or independent activities. Your class will enjoy the assortment of supplies, and your store of materials will be easier to organize.

Mary Dinneen—Gr. 2, Mountain View School, Bristol, CT

Super Filing System

How often have you come across an idea in a magazine, copied it, and then were uncertain where to file it? Many times an idea can be used in several curricu-lum areas, and it is difficult to pinpoint which subject or theme it would best be filed under. Why not make several copies of the idea; then place a copy in several dif-ferent folders? The idea may describe a good science activity, but would also work well in a literature unit. With a copy of the idea under each heading, you'll be sure to come across it as you plan for a unit of study.

Nancy Bauer—Gr. 2, Kidwell Elementary School, Iowa Park, TX

Favorite Books

As you use special literature during the school year, file each book in your monthly ac-tivity folder. After sharing a story with the class, make sure the book is placed with your sea-sonal curriculum material instead of on the classroom library shelf. If using a book bor-rowed from the school or public library, write down the title and author and slip the informa-tion into your files. You'll be pleased to have the book on hand for the next year, instead of trying to track it down somewhere in your classroom!

VaReane Heese
Springfield Elementary
Omaha, NE

Student Folder Tip

If your supply list includes prong folders and notebook paper, this timesaving idea will help organize materials before they even get to school! Add a note to the supply list asking parents to insert 25 sheets of notebook paper into each folder. The folders can also be labeled with the student's name and the designated subject area. If you request a specific color for each folder, include that information on your note as well. When students arrive on the first day, the folders will be organized and ready to go.

The Second-Grade Teachers, Lincoln School, Baxter Spring, KS

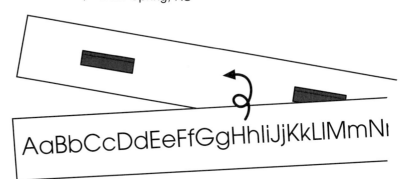

An Attractive Idea

Desktop alphabet strips and number lines are subjected to a lot of wear and tear throughout the school year. To keep these items looking as good as new, laminate the strips for durability; then attach a length of magnetic tape to the back side of each strip. Students can store the strips on the metal areas underneath their desks. When needed, the strips are easily accessible. With a little care, these supplies will last all year long!

Sr. Sandra Krupp—Gr. 1, Sacred Heart Private School, Bronx, NY

Word Books

Word cards are a great tool for teaching beginning sight words, but making individual sets and keeping track of all the cards are time-consuming chores. Simplify the situation by requesting that each student obtain a hardback composition notebook. As sight words and reading vocabulary are introduced, type a word list in large print. Duplicate a copy of the list for each student to glue in his word book. Students will have easy access to all the vocabulary that has been introduced throughout the year without trying to manage a cumbersome stack of cards. The books can also be taken home for extra practice.

Betty Silkunas—Gr. 1
Oak Lane Day School
Blue Bell, PA

Learning-Center Storage

Make learning centers more attractive and fun to use with creative containers. Recycle unusual containers to house special activities and game pieces, letting the type of container inspire new ways to program skills. A round ice-cream container can hold cone-shaped cutouts with the names of ice-cream flavors to alphabetize. A metal bandage box can store vocabulary cards featuring first-aid terms. An animal-cracker box becomes a container for facts about endangered animals. With such attractive packaging, students will be eager to explore the learning-center activities.

VaReane Heese, Springfield Elementary, Omaha, NE

Student File Box

Help each student stay organized with an inexpensive, individual file box. Ask each student to bring a large, empty cereal box to school. Cut each box to resemble a magazine file. Provide paints and markers for students to decorate their boxes. Attach a label to the front of each box for each student to neatly print his name. Arrange the completed boxes in alphabetical order; then staple the boxes together side by side to form one large filing system. This will serve as a place for students to store completed paperwork and important notes. At the end of each day, remind students to check their boxes for items that need to go home. Desks will stay much neater with this organized way to keep track of papers!

Betty Silkunas—Gr. 1, Oak Lane Day School, Blue Bell, PA

Laundry-Basket Storage

When it comes to organizing bulky items, don't overlook the laundry basket for storing materials. A plastic laundry basket is perfect for holding playground balls and jump ropes, carrying a class supply of lunchboxes for a field trip, and helping organize books on library day. The basket's handles and lightweight material make it easy for students to carry. When the baskets are not in use, they can be stacked and stored under a table. For such a low-cost item, you'll be amazed at its versatility in the classroom!

Mary Dinneen—Gr. 2, Mountain View School, Bristol, CT

Alarming Reminder

Johnny needs to leave for speech, Susie needs to take her medicine, Bobby has to leave for a dentist appointment—all at different times throughout the day! To help keep on top of special situations, invest in a travel alarm clock. Set the clock each morning so the alarm will remind you when someone needs to leave the classroom. The clock can be reset to keep up with the comings and goings of all your students. When the alarm goes off, you'll be reminded to get everyone headed in the right direction on time.

Susan Wilson—Gr. 1, Sevierville Elementary, Sevierville, TN

Work In Progress

Eliminate lost papers with this system for unfinished work. Create a folder or a file tray labeled "Work In Progress." When a student has an incomplete assignment, he places his paper in the folder. When he has free time or a study period, the student checks the folder to see if there is work he needs to complete. At the end of the day, send any papers still "in progress" home with the student to complete as homework. Unfinished work won't end up lost in desks or be forgotten when students have this system to keep them on the right track.

Mary Jo Kampschnieder, Howells Community Catholic Schools, Howells, NE

Desktop Organizer

A rectangular plastic basket can hold all the supplies that students need on hand during a busy school day. Place each basket between two desktops so that the contents are shared by two students. Fill each basket with a travel-size box of tissues, two red grading pens, two sharpened pencils, and a large pencil eraser. Students will no longer need to get up during a lesson to get a tissue, or dig through their supply boxes in search of a pencil. Items in the basket can be restocked at the end of the day, assuring that the supplies will be ready and waiting the following morning.

Vicki O'Neal—Gr. 2
Lincoln School
Baxter Springs, KS

Instant Bookshelves

Be on the lookout for a greeting-card stand that can be recycled into a bookshelf for your classroom. Greeting-card and stationery shops periodically change the display stands and are often willing to donate them for classroom use. Some stands come with drawers in the bottom, which come in handy for storing unused books. Students enjoy browsing this display for independent reading choices, and you'll love the organization it brings to your classroom.

Nancy Bauer—Gr. 2
Kidwell Elementary
Iowa Park, TX

 August

 Class Rules

 Homework Policy

 Supply List

 Welcome Back Letters

 Welcome Back 1

 Welcome Back 2

Computer Correspondence

Make the most of computer technology by creating monthly folders to hold information that is used year after year. A file for August can hold your welcome letter, homework policy, and supply list. September's file can keep track of references needed for your Johnny Appleseed unit and activities used on Grandparents Day. Class lists and a copy of the daily schedule can be kept in a master folder. As the year goes by, you'll know exactly where to find the documents to print out and send home.

VaReane Heese
Springfield Elementary
Omaha, NE

Reteaching Folder

Keep track of the students who need one-on-one help and papers that need to be corrected with a folder that stays right by your grade book. As you are correcting assignments, place papers with unsatisfactory grades into the folder as soon as they have been graded. This folder will serve as a reminder to meet with the student and give him immediate feedback on skills that need to be retaught. Check the folder every day to make sure you are addressing problems as soon as they come to your attention. Students will appreciate the quick response to their work, and you'll stay on top of student progress.

Nancy Bauer—Gr. 2, Kidwell Elementary, Iowa Park, TX

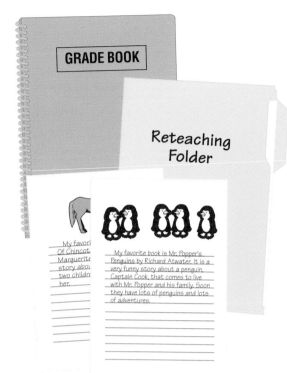

Absentee Assignments

Have you ever had trouble collecting assignments for students who are absent? Prepare several folders for such an occasion and you'll be amazed at the ease of organizing missed work. Decorate several file folders with stickers or markers and label each one "We Missed You!" If desired, laminate the folders for durability. When a student is absent, place a folder on his desk. Ask the student who sits next to the empty desk to be in charge of placing in the folder a copy of all handouts, workbook pages, and notes to go home. Any textbooks used during the day should be placed on the empty desk as well. When someone comes to pick up the absent student's assignments, everything the student needs will be organized and sitting on top of his desk. What a time-saver!

Susan Wilson—Gr. 1
Sevierville Elementary
Sevierville, TN

Magnetic Message Board

Let your metal filing cabinet serve double duty by using it as a message board. Keep a supply of magnetic message holders on hand and use them to display notes, lists, and memos that need your immediate attention. Make sure to look over the messages each morning as you come into the classroom, and again before you leave for the day. Important messages won't be misplaced or escape your attention when you have them displayed in this handy way.

Nancy Bauer—Gr. 2
Kidwell Elementary School
Iowa Park, TX

Auxiliary Plan Book

Help organize your plan book a year in advance with this easy system. When you select a plan book for the current year, pick up an extra book for advance planning. As you plan your lessons for the current year, make notes and list details you want to remember for the next time you teach a certain lesson or outline new themes for future use. Jot down the information on self-stick notes and attach to the extra book to ensure that you remember the information in the future. You might want to remember to teach tangrams in September instead of April, to list the titles of library books that worked well in your solar-system unit, or to make a note to request a seasonal video before it is in demand. At the end of the year, your "empty" plan book will be full of tips to make the next year run smoothly.

Mary Dinneen—Gr. 2
Mountain View School
Bristol, CT

17

GETTING ACQUAINTED

Double Duty

To prepare for this get-acquainted activity, think of things that go together. Create picture or word cards of items that come in sets of two, featuring each item of the pair on a separate card. (For example, make a card with a picture of salt and another card with pepper, and a card with ice cream and another with cake.) Be sure to have one card for each student in your class. Distribute a card to each student; then instruct the class to find the other half of their pairs. When students have made a match, have them introduce themselves to each other before handing their cards to you. Redistribute the cards for another round of play. Your students will get along just like peas and carrots!

VaReane Heese, Springfield Elementary, Omaha, NE

Tasty Introductions

Create a nonthreatening way for students to introduce themselves with this taste-tempting approach. Invite students to sit in a circle as they share information about themselves. Place a jar filled with pretzels, crackers, or other small treats in the center of the circle. Ask a question such as "How old are you?" or "What is your favorite part of the school day?" As each student volunteers an answer, he may take a treat from the jar. Students will be eager to tell about themselves in such friendly surroundings.

Kelly Wong—Gr. 2, Berlyn School, Ontario, CA

Gift-Bag Greeting

Help new students feel especially welcome on their first day by having a gift bag waiting on each desk. Fill a plastic, zippered bag for each student with a ball of play dough, a cookie cutter, and an art activity. Shy, uncertain students will feel comforted by the activities, and outgoing students can busy themselves with the contents while you greet other students at the door. The gift bag will also occupy the students while you take attendance, check in materials, and prepare for the next activity. This welcome gift is a treat for everyone!

Linda Parris—Gr. 1
West Hills Elementary School, Knoxville, TN

Musical Circles

Gather your students 'round for a musical way to meet one another. Divide your class into two equal groups. Have one group form a circle with the students facing outward. Instruct the other group to form an outer circle around the first group, with the students facing the center of the circle. Play a short musical selection while the inner circle walks clockwise and the outer circle walks counterclockwise. When the music stops, the students halt and introduce themselves to the student they are now facing. Continue playing until students have had a chance to become acquainted with several classmates. What a way to get things started on the right note!

Sarah Mertz, Owenton, KY

Draw, Partner!

Invite students to use those brand-new crayons as they team up for this artistic introduction activity. Distribute a sheet of drawing paper to each student; then pair everyone with a partner. Instruct each student to draw a picture of her partner and learn one thing about her to share with the class. When the illustrations are complete, have each student stand with her partner while she shows her picture to the class and announces, "This is my new friend, [name], and one thing I know about her is...." Display the portraits for students to enjoy throughout the school day; then allow each student to take home her likeness.

Susan Wilson—Gr. 1, Sevierville Elementary, Sevierville, TN

19

Name Game

Sometimes it's difficult for students to learn the names of their new classmates, but this game will make it easy *and* fun. Write each student's name on a separate piece of paper and place the names in a basket or container. Throughout the day, draw out a student's name and give her the opportunity to identify five students in the classroom by name. Award the effort with a sticker or small prize. Make sure to give everyone a chance to participate during the day, and by dismissal time everyone will be on a first-name basis!

Nancy Bauer—Gr. 2
Kidwell Elementary
Iowa Park, TX

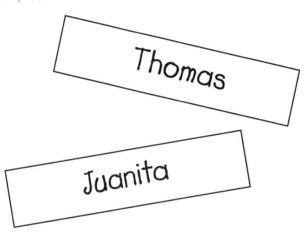

Classmate-In-A-Box

During the first week of school, ask students to begin gathering special mementos and objects that are representative of themselves. These items are to be placed in a specially decorated shoebox and shared with the class during a get-acquainted show-and-tell at the end of the week. Encourage students to look for items such as photos, vacation souvenirs, awards, and collectibles. After showing their boxes to the class, have students look for classmates with similar items or objects that show a common interest. If desired, keep the boxes on display for an Open House exhibit.

Lori Sammartino
Clayton Traditional Academy
Pittsburgh, PA

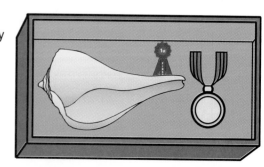

I Spy…A New Friend!

Introductions are more fun if a mystery is involved! Have students learn the names of their new classmates with a round of I Spy, using clues leading to introductions. The teacher begins by describing a student she spies in the classroom, while the students try to guess the identity. When the identity of the student has been confirmed, the student stands and announces, "Hi, my name is _____." The class responds by using the student's name as they return the greeting. The game continues with the student using the I Spy format to give a description of another student in the class. Who spies a great way to break the ice?

Nancy Bauer—Gr. 2
Kidwell Elementary
Iowa Park, TX

In The Spotlight

Create a special setting for getting acquainted by putting your students in the spotlight. Dim the lights in your classroom and have a flashlight handy. Ask a question such as "How do you get to school?" or "What is your favorite subject?" Call on each student to answer by focusing the flashlight's beam on him. After several questions have been answered, let each student take center stage as you direct the flashlight on him and ask the class for information they have learned about the student. This enlightening activity will have students familiar with each other in no time!

Nancy Bauer—Gr. 2

Name Bingo

Help students get to know one another with a game of name-calling—on bingo cards! Duplicate a class set of the blank bingo-card pattern on page 74. Distribute a card and a supply of bingo chips to each student. Instruct him to ask fellow classmates to sign their names in empty squares of the card. When everyone has a full card, call out student names in place of traditional bingo numbers. When a student has a bingo, have him call out the names he covered on his card. As he calls out each name, have that student stand up by his desk. Play several rounds, making sure each student's name has been called. Classmates will learn one another's names in no time at all!

Kelly Wong—Gr. 2
Berlyn School
Ontario, CA

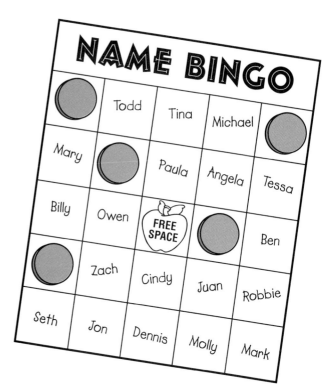

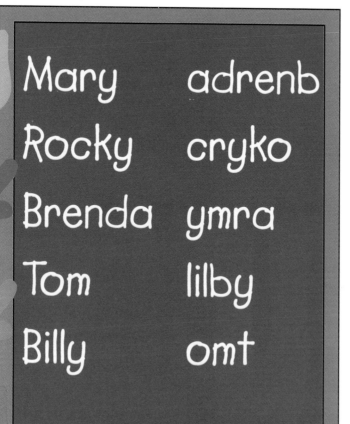

Scrambled Names

This little mix-up will help students become familiar with one another on the first day of school. Write a list of your students' first names on the chalkboard. Create a second column and list the names again, but this time rearrange the order of the names *and* the letters in each name. Ask students to refer to the first column as they try to unscramble the spelling of each name in the second column. If desired, have students record their answers on pieces of paper. Allow time for students to complete the activity; then ask each student to come to the board and point out his scrambled name before introducing himself to the class. Students will have one another's names straight before you know it!

Doris Hautala—Gr. 3
Washington Elementary
Ely, MN

Literary Introductions

Let a good book help your students learn more about one another. A few weeks before the big day arrives, send a letter to each of your new students asking him to bring a favorite book with him on the first day of school. Use a show-and-tell format to have each student introduce himself and show his book to the class. Ask the student to share something about the book and show an illustration to the class. If desired, have students keep the books at school for the first few weeks, and select a book each day for storytime. Not only will students get to know one another, they will also share the love of a good book!

adapted from an idea by Betty Silkunas—Gr. 1, Oak Lane Day School, Blue Bell, PA

Show-And-Tell Nametags

These impressive nametags are a great way for students to share information about themselves. Duplicate a class set of the nametag pattern on page 75 onto tagboard or heavy paper. Distribute a nametag to each student and instruct him to complete each section with the requested information. Assist each student in pinning the completed project to his shirt, or use a hole puncher and a length of yarn to create a medallion for the student to wear. Then encourage students to peruse their classmates' nametags, discussing the similarities and differences among themselves. If desired, save the projects for a bulletin-board display for Open House or Parent Night. What a lot of mileage from a simple nametag!

Mary Jo Kampschnieder
Howells Community Catholic Schools, Howells, NE

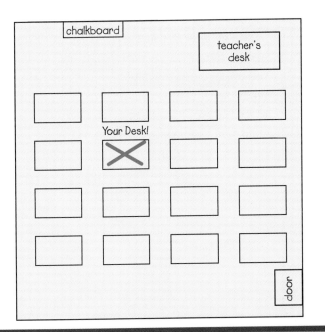

Welcome Map

As you greet your new students on the first day of school, present each child with a classroom map. Each map should show the class seating arrangement and have a large X placed on top of a different desk. Encourage each student to use his map to locate the designated desk, where he will find a marker and a blank nametag waiting for him to fill it out. When all students have arrived and settled in, help each student affix his nametag to his desk. With these activities in line, students will find their way to a great beginning!

Doris Hautala—Gr. 3
Washington Elementary, Ely, MN

Routines

Counting The Days

Extend the morning calendar routine with an activity that will have students counting the days. After the new date has been added to the calendar, keep track of its order in the school year by numbering a cutout shape for each day. If desired, use a shape symbolic of the current month to record each day. September's cutout could be an apple shape, followed by a pumpkin cutout for October and a turkey shape for November. Arrange the daily cutouts in a row across the top of the classroom wall. If desired, display the name of the month and season under the cutouts of each shape. The resulting display will provide a number line, the names of the months and seasons, and a countdown to the 100th day of school.

Dianne G. Thompson—Special Education
Avondale Elementary School
Birmingham, AL

Partner Pair-Up

Have this simple pairing-up strategy ready for the first day of class. Divide your class list into two equal groups. Write each student's name on a craft stick, using a different-colored marker for each group of students. Place each group's sticks in its own decorative cup or can. When you're ready to pair students for an activity, pull one name from each can to create a set of partners. The students are randomly paired and ready to work!

Kathleen N. Kopp
Lecanto Primary School
Lecanto, FL

What's For Lunch?

Use the school lunch menu for a morning routine that promotes oral reading skills and boosts self-esteem. Before taking the daily lunch count, select a student to read the lunch menu to the class. (If desired, select a student at the end of the day to read the next day's menu. Send home a copy of the menu so that the student can practice reading it.) Not only will your students gain practice speaking before the class, but it will also answer the often-asked question, "What's for lunch?"

Rosemary Linden
Royal Valley Elementary School
Hoyt, KS

Calendar Cash

Use your classroom calendar to help reinforce money skills. Gather a supply of pennies, dimes, and a dollar bill, and attach a small piece of Velcro® to the back of each coin and bill. As students change the date each day, have them add a penny to an accumulative counting board. To make the board, attach four strips of Velcro® to a piece of oaktag. Mount the board next to the calendar. With the arrival of each new day, a student places a penny on a Velcro® strip. When 10 pennies appear on the board, they are traded in for a dime. When 10 dimes have accumulated, they are exchanged for a dollar bill. As counting skills are mastered, nickels can be added to the activity. Your students are not only marking the passage of time, but also strengthening their skills in counting money.

Joan Costello—Gr. 1
William McGinn School
Scotch Plains, NJ

Learning Logs

Students will reinforce skills and content as they share their school day with parents with this nightly journal assignment. Provide each student with a journal to use as his "Learning Log." Each evening, the student tells his parents about something he learned in school that day. Together the parent and child make a journal entry telling about the learning. Emphasize the importance of writing about what the student *learned* as opposed to listing what the student *did* that day. As you review each student's Learning Log, you will be able to better assess his understanding of the curriculum. Parents will be able to evaluate the learning, too, when they take part in this nightly routine.

Lori Sammartino
Clayton Traditional Academy
Pittsburgh, PA

September 28
Today I learned that some animals hibernate in the winter.

MONDAY 1
TUESDAY 2
WEDNESDAY 3
THURSDAY 4
FRIDAY 5

A Dozen Ways To Get In Line

Reinforce basic skills and knowledge when it's time for your class to line up. Instruct students to line up by:

- alphabetical order of their first names
- alphabetical order of their surnames
- months of their birthdays
- dates of their birthdays
- colors of shirts
- colors of pants
- numerical order of the last two digits of their phone numbers
- numerical order of their street addresses
- seasons in which they were born
- alphabetical order of their street names
- number of brothers or sisters they have
- number of buttons on their clothing

Terry Healy—Gifted K–6
Eugene Field Elementary
Manhattan, KS

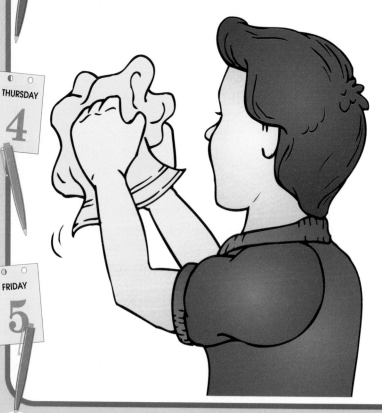

Scrub Schedule

Hand-washing can be a time-consuming process when the whole class is trying to clean up for computer lab, for lunchtime, or after an art project. Speed up the process by tearing an old towel into washcloth-size pieces and placing them in a bucket near the sink. When it's time for a quick cleanup, pour warm, soapy water over the cloths. Distribute a cloth to each student. After cleaning his hands, the student drops his cloth back into the bucket. Take the bucket home and launder the cloths at the end of each day. Cleanup is complete in no time at all.

Mary Dinneen—Gr. 2
Mountain View School
Bristol, CT

Watch Me Grow!

Keep a pictorial record of your students as they grow and change during the school year. Display a large measurement chart by your classroom calendar. Have each student stand by the chart as you take her picture on the first day of school. Repeat the process at various times of the year, making sure to include both the calendar and chart in the picture. At the end of the year, distribute the photos for each child to take home and share with her parents. It's amazing to see how much each child has grown!

Mary Jo Kampschnieder
Howells Community Catholic School
Howells, NE

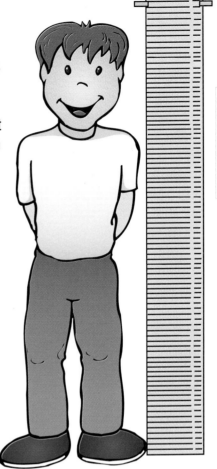

Student V.I.P.'s

Building your students' self-esteem can become part of your regular classroom routine. Create a hallway display to honor each student as V.I.P. for a week. As a student's turn to be the V.I.P. arrives, have him create a poster with information about his birthday, place of birth, favorite food, and other personal information. While he is working on the poster, instruct the other students to compose notes with positive comments about the honored student. If desired, have the class conduct an interview with the V.I.P. as you take notes. Compile the interview information into a newspaper-type article about the student, and display it with the poster and notes. Finally take a picture of the student standing by the handiwork. Self-esteem will soar to great heights as students are recognized as being super-special people!

Vicki O'Neal—Gr. 2, Lincoln School
Baxter Springs, KS

Clothespin Record-Keeper

This simple routine will take care of attendance and lunch count with one quick step. To set up the system, you will need a class supply of spring-type clothespins, a sheet of poster board, scissors, and a permanent marker. Cut a large circle from the poster board; then use the marker to visually divide the circle into three equal sections. Label each section with one of the following categories: "Buying Lunch," "Brought My Lunch," and "Gone For The Day." Mount the circle on a bulletin board or an other place that students can easily reach. Then print each student's name on a clothespin and clip it to the section titled "Gone For The Day." When each student arrives at school in the morning, she removes her clothespin from that section and clips it to the correct lunch category. With a quick glance at the wheel, you'll be able to tell which students are absent and how many are buying lunch. At the end of the day, each student clips his clothespin to the "Gone For The Day" section. Everything will be ready to go for another day.

Joan Costello—Gr. 1, William McGinn School
Scotch Plains, NJ

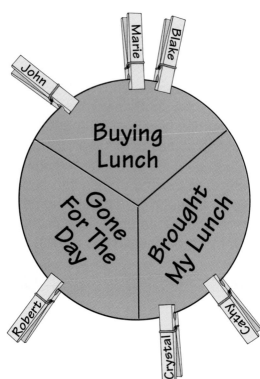

water plants
collect papers
line leader
lunch-ticket taker
calendar monitor

Josh

Jason

Carlos

Tanna

Mike

Melissa

Rebecca

Emma

Class Job Chart

Keep track of classroom duties with a simple color-coding system. Create a class list on poster board or chart paper, and display it on a bulletin board. Use a colored pushpin and matching label to represent each classroom job. For example, use the green pin for the plant monitor, the blue pin for the line leader, and the yellow pin for the lunch-ticket taker. As a student is assigned a duty in the classroom, place the appropriate pushpin by the name on the chart. The pins are easily moved from name to name as jobs are rotated. With this system, keeping track of student helpers is the easiest job of all!

VaReane Heese
Springfield Elementary
Omaha, NE

Classroom Agenda

Ensure that everyone is in-the-know about your classroom routine by creating a poster-size copy of your schedule. List the time and subject for each period of the school day, making note of any special activities and the days they occur. Students can refer to the schedule during the day to help remember library times, music class, or recess. Substitutes will appreciate the visual reference as they try to stick as closely to the typical routine as possible. When every minute of the school day counts, this handy schedule can keep things right on track.

Kelly A. Wong—Gr. 2
Berlyn School
Ontario, CA

8:00–8:45	Attendance/Flag/Calendar
8:45–9:30	Math
9:30–10:00	Journal & Sharing
10:00–10:20	Recess
10:20–12:00	Arts & Crafts

Shape Groups

Create a routine for organizing small groups with the use of decorative hole punchers. Use a different-shaped punch for each group you wish to create. Punch a shape onto an index card for each student in the class. Distribute one card to each student; then have students with like shapes work together. Cards can be collected and used again, or can be used for writing a message to each student praising his group's effort.

This method can also be used to regulate groups at center time. Construct a larger version of each shape and post one shape at each center. Students with a matching shape card may work at the center that day.

VaReane Heese
Springfield Elementary
Omaha, NE

Cody

Gina

Jerry

MONDAY 1

TUESDAY 2

WEDNESDAY 3

THURSDAY 4

FRIDAY 5

PARENT COMMUNICATION

First-Day Newsletter

All parents are eager to hear about their child's first day of school. Try writing a short class newsletter to tell parents about the day's exciting events. Set aside a few minutes near the end of the day to list the day's activities. Duplicate a copy of the newsletter for each child to take home and add an individual note on each one. Parents will be so delighted at this chance to learn about their youngster's day, they'll feel as if they were there, too!

Betty Silkunas—Gr. 1, Oak Lane Day School, Blue Bell, PA

Take Note!

Looking for a way to send important notices home with students? Then try this tip! Write short messages on address labels and attach them to students' hands. For example, if a parent is supposed to send napkins for a class party, simply write "napkins" and the date they are needed on an address label. Students will enjoy this unique method of taking home messages and parents will appreciate the reminder.

Kelly A. Wong—Gr. 2, Berlyn School, Ontario, CA

Napkins Needed Tomorrow

Stamp-Pad Communication

This small investment can be a big help in communicating with parents. Purchase a date stamp and two different colors of ink pads to use when sending home papers. One color of ink will indicate the current date to let parents know when a paper was handed out. The other color is used for stamping a due date on homework, book orders, or correspondence that needs to be returned to school. This method will be a great help to parents when students take home several papers at once—the parent can easily make note of when assignments were given to the student and when they are expected to be completed.

Nancy Bauer—Gr. 2, Kidwell Elementary, Iowa Park, TX

October 23

FIELD TRIP PERMISSION SLIP

Christy
student's name

_____
parent's signature
October 28

In The News

Make each week a newsworthy occasion with a classroom newsletter for parents. Each week, duplicate one copy of the open newsletter on page 76. Spend a few minutes each day jotting down the daily activities and skills that were covered. At the end of the week, add information about upcoming projects, field trips, and any other needed reminders. Be sure to also include ideas for reinforcing the week's skills at home, book reviews of the latest children's literature, and exciting websites on the Internet. Then duplicate a copy for each child. If desired, attach activity sheets that parents can do with their children. Parents will appreciate being kept up-to-date with newsletters that are hot off the presses!

Nicole Iacovazzi—Gr. 3, Owego Elementary, Vestal, NY

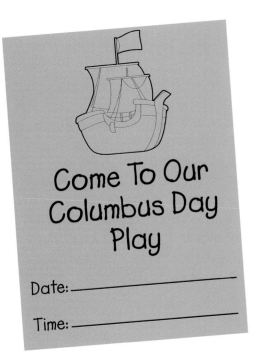

Neon Notes

At the beginning of the school year, parents receive notes, notes, and more notes! Try this tip to make your note to parents stick out from the rest. After composing a letter to parents explaining classroom procedures and policies, duplicate a class supply of the letters on a neon color of copy paper. As parents look through the many notes sent home the first week of school, they will immediately be drawn to your letter. Continue to use this same color of paper on all homebound notices throughout the year. Whenever parents see this bright color, they'll know the note is from you and therefore worthy of reading!

Kathleen M. Geddes Darby—Gr. 1
Community School
Cumberland, RI

A Knack For Snacks

Send the message that snacktime at school should be a nutritious affair. Have students create a newsletter with lists and illustrations of healthful snacks for parents to send to school. If desired, include a recipe or two that tie(s) in to a unit of study. Not only will the snacks provide an energy boost for hardworking students; they will also remind parents that healthful eating habits play an important role in their child's development.

Diane Outlaw—Gr. 1
Fabra Elementary
Boerne, TX

Reading Calendar

This reading plan makes reading a family affair! Duplicate a class supply of calendar sheets for the first month of school, or use the blank calendar form on page 77. In a parent letter, explain that the goal of the reading plan is for the child to read or be read to for a specified number of minutes per day. When the daily goal is met, the parent initials the corresponding calendar space. At the end of the month, have students return their calendars to school and take home a new calendar. Encourage students to read books associated with current themes and authors being studied by listing them at the bottom of each month's calendar. Not only are students increasing their reading skills, but they're also spending high-quality time with their parents. What a great combination!

Kathleen M. Geddes Darby—Gr. 1, Community School, Cumberland, RI

Note Folders

With this simple plan, each child will receive a positive note to take home each month of school. Personalize a file folder for each student; then label the inside of each folder with the school-year months. Place a variety of writing paper in each child's folder, such as school letterhead, notebook paper, postcards, notepads, stationery, and sticky notes. Each day write a note to the parents of a different student. Record your comments in that month's space on each child's folder and then send the note home. By the end of the month, you'll know that each child has received a note during the past few weeks and you're ready to begin the process again. The folders are also great for recording correspondence received from parents.

Sarah Mertz, Owenton, KY

Video Tour

Since many working parents are not able to visit your classroom, why not send the classroom home to them? Ask a friend or colleague to make a videotape of you as you state your expectations for the new year, explain your grading policy, and discuss the class schedule. Also include footage of the classroom, with explanations about learning centers and ongoing projects. This tape can be sent home with a different child each afternoon for the first few weeks of school. The tape will also come in handy as new students join your class throughout the year.

Nancy Bauer—Gr. 2, Kidwell Elementary, Iowa Park, TX

Proud As A Peacock

For a twist on traditional show-and-tell, give parents an opportunity to share a proud moment about their child. Each week, send home copies of the "Proud As A Peacock!" form on page 78 with several students. When the parents receive the form, they are to jot down a reason they are proud of their child, then send the form back to school the next day. Start off the morning by calling on a student to read his "Proud As A Peacock" note to the class. Students will beam with pride as they report the good news their parents have written. Since each child will take home the form several times during the year, encourage them to ask grandparents, aunts, and uncles to participate!

Susan Wilson—Gr. 1
Sevierville Elementary
Sevierville, TN

Proud As A Peacock!

We are very proud of __Tammy Benita__
because __she cleaned up__
__her room all by__
__herself.__

Date: __March 15__
Signed: __Mrs. Benita__

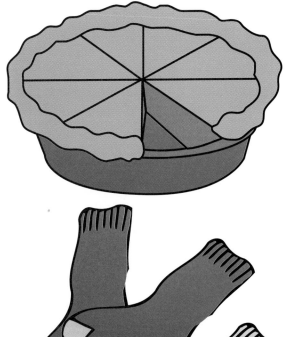

Family Math Night

Host a family math night early in the school year to demonstrate how parents can reinforce math skills at home. Explain to parents that many household activities can become springboards for learning. A pile of socks on laundry day can lead to an activity with sorting and classifying; cutting a pie after dinner can promote a discussion on fractions or equal shares. Provide "household" manipulatives—such as dry beans, pennies, dry cereal, newspaper ads, and coupons—and show how these items can aid in solving math problems. Remind parents that many children's games reinforce counting, number recognition, and problem-solving strategies. As parents become more familiar with math strategies, they will find many new ways to reinforce the concepts at home.

Diane Outlaw—Gr. 1
Fabra Elementary
Boerne, TX

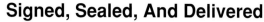

Signed, Sealed, And Delivered

Here's a great and inexpensive way to help children get important notices home on time and in recognizable form. Use a permanent marker to write students' names on large, plastic resealable bags. Inform parents that papers requiring immediate attention will be carried in these bags. Students place notices and letters to their parents inside their plastic bags and then seal the bags. When students get home from school, they remove the papers from the bags and return the bags to school the following day. The bags are also great for parents to return signed notes and other correspondence to the teacher. Now all pieces of home- and school-bound correspondence are sure to arrive on time and in good condition.

Victoria A. Cavanagh—Gr. 3
Troy Hills School
Parsippany, NJ

Documentation Solution

Eliminate documentation dilemmas with this convenient system. Personalize a file folder for each child. When parents send notes to school, file them in the appropriate folder. Before sending personal notes home to parents, be sure to make copies of the notes on a copy machine or with carbon paper. Then place the copies of the notes in each child's folder. Not only will all correspondence be organized, but you'll also have documentation at your fingertips if questions arise about dates or messages.

Nancy Bauer—Gr. 2, Kidwell Elementary, Iowa Park, TX

Thanks For Sharing!

Keep a camera handy for those special moments when students earn an award, get new glasses, wear a special outfit, or reach an individual goal. Send the parent one of the photos along with a note thanking them for sharing their child with you. Students will burst with pride as they take these notes home, and parents will be thrilled at the special attention you have shown.

Rosemary Linden, Royal Valley Elementary School, Hoyt, KS

Noteworthy News

Preprogramming positive notes with your students' names eliminates time-consuming record-keeping. Purchase a different decorative notepad for each month of the school year. Personalize a page from each notepad for every student. Each day tear off the top page on that month's notepad and jot a positive note to that child. For an added treat, tape a piece of wrapped candy to the note before giving it to the child. The student will know the note is of a positive nature and one his parents will be proud to receive. When you run out of personalized pages in a notepad, you'll know that each child has received a note of praise during the past few weeks. Then retrieve the next month's notepad and begin the process again!

Sarah Mertz, Owenton, KY

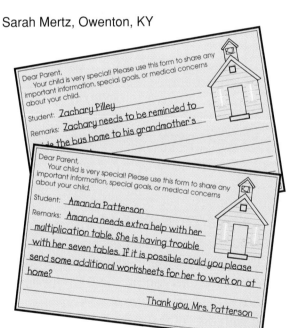

Getting Acquainted

Encourage parent-teacher communication by giving parents the opportunity to tell you about their child. Duplicate a copy of the information form on page 79 for each student. Place a copy of the form in each child's registration or beginning-of-the-year packet. Parents will appreciate the opportunity to inform you of medical or academic problems, emotional concerns, or family situations they feel are important for you to know. After reading each child's form, file this valuable student information for future reference.

Susan Wilson—Gr. 1
Sevierville Elementary
Sevierville, TN

Homework Helps

Send parents a few tips for making at-home learning more enjoyable for both parent and child. Suggest key phrasing for making homework help more productive, such as "Show me how you got your answer," or "Can you read the directions to me?" Explain that students will feel less frustrated when help is offered in a constructive manner. Also include ideas for helping students follow printed text from left to right, and using bedtime stories for reinforcement of predicting story outcomes and identifying characters and settings. Parents will appreciate your input on making learning a more pleasurable family experience.

Diane Outlaw—Gr. 1, Fabra Elementary, Boerne, TX

Positive Reinforcement

School Rule Book

Familiarize students with your classroom rules by creating individual rule booklets. In advance, type each class rule on a separate sheet of paper and duplicate a set for each student. As you discuss each rule with your class, have each student draw a picture in her booklet to illustrate the rule. Staple together the completed pages so that each student has her own booklet. Encourage students to take the books home to review with their parents. When it comes to classroom behavior, your students will see the big picture!

Kelly A. Wong—Gr. 2
Berlyn School
Ontario, CA

Raise your hand
before you speak.

Be considerate.

Work quietly.

Keys To A Good Year

Get students all keyed up for good behavior with this incentive for following classroom rules. Use the pattern on page 80 to duplicate a supply of key-shaped cutouts. Program each key with one of the classroom rules. When you see a student modeling good behavior, award him with a key cutout citing the rule that he followed. The key shape can be pinned to the student's shirt, or threaded on a piece of yarn and worn as a medallion. If desired, enlarge several key patterns and list a class rule on each one for use in a display titled "Keys For Good Behavior."

VaReane Heese
Springfield Elementary
Omaha, NE

Math whiz

Good Job!

You're special!

Super Student!

You're terrific!

Weekly Behavior Log

Students will feel more accountable for their behavior when they keep a daily record of their actions. At the beginning of each month, supply each student with a copy of the blank calendar on page 77. Help students label the name of the month and write the correct date in each square of the calendar. At the end of each day, instruct each student to use the calendar to jot down any behavioral problems he had during the day, such as "too much talking" or "pushing in line." At the end of each week, have students evaluate their conduct. Provide a small reward for students who demonstrated outstanding conduct, and offer a note of encouragement to those who have shown improvement. Students can take their calendars home at the end of the month so that parents are aware of classroom conduct, too.

Kelly A. Wong—Gr. 2
Berlyn School
Ontario, CA

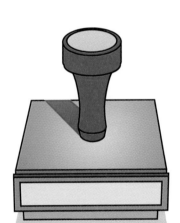

Positive Postings

Have a positive reinforcement ready whenever you need it with this quick and easy tip. Without pulling the pages apart, stamp each page of a self-sticking notepad with a positive message such as "I'm proud of you!" or "Good job!" When you want to give a quick reward for keeping a clean desk or following the rules, simply pull a stamped page from the pad and stick it to the student's desk. If desired, let students redeem the notes at the end of the day for a treat. With this supply of notes on hand, you'll never miss the opportunity to reinforce good behavior.

Nancy Bauer—Gr. 2
Kidwell Elementary
Iowa Park, TX

Die-Cut Delights

Create unique student rewards using a die-cut shape and a variety of materials. Cut shapes from sandpaper, cardboard, corrugated paper, felt, or wallpaper scraps. Write a positive message on the resulting cutout; then attach a small safety pin to the back. When a student's behavior is worthy of notice, reward her with a die-cut badge to honor her success. Students will proudly bear the messages of their award-winning conduct.

VaReane Heese
Springfield Elementary
Omaha, NE

You're The Apple Of My Eye!

name

Keep Up The Good Work!

Apple Of Your Eye

You'll have a bushel of super students with this system for rewarding good behavior. Create a supply of apple certificates using the pattern on page 81. Each time a student models successful conduct, award him with a certificate applauding his behavior. Provide a special learning-center activity or some recess equipment for students who have earned an apple during the day. It won't be long before you have a crop of model students!

Beverly Langland
Trinity Christian Academy
Jacksonville, FL

Bang-Up Jobs

Keep a supply of special rewards on hand for student who demonstrate a bang-up job. Purchase a bag of the miniature-size Lifesaver® candy rolls. Thread a pipe cleaner through the center of each roll. Fold over one end of the pipe cleaner to keep it in place. Attach red curly ribbon to the extended end to resemble a lighted firecracker. When a student does an exceptional job on a test or an assignment, present her with a fireworks treat along with a note proclaiming, "You did a bang-up job!" Parents will appreciate the encouraging note, and the treats will be a big hit with the students!

Rosemary Linden
Royal Valley Elementary
Hoyt, KS

Pocketful Of Reinforcement

As the holidays near and excitement builds, you may need extra incentives to keep students on task. Keep plenty of encouragement within reach with a reward apron. Buy or make an apron with lots of pockets sewn in. Fill the pockets with stickers, candies, pencils and other small surprises. When students are in need of positive reinforcement, tie on the apron and look for students who are working quietly. Reward this good behavior by letting those students choose something from a pocket. Students will soon learn to be on their best behavior when they see you putting on the apron. What a treat for everyone!

Nancy Bauer—Gr. 2
Kidwell Elementary
Iowa Park, TX

Clean-Desk Awards

Help promote a roomful of tidy desks with a special reward for those who keep things neat. Use shape pads that represent a symbol of the current month to write a positive message about the neatness of the desk. Compose a message that correlates with the month, such as "Good Apple Desk Award" for September, or "I'm thankful for your neat desk" in November. Place the award inside each tidy desk while the students are out of the room. If desired, leave a small reward such as a sticker or treat with the message. Students will make an effort to keep their desks in order when they know you'll be sneaking a peek inside!

Vicki O'Neal—Gr. 2
Lincoln School
Baxter Springs, KS

ART PROJECTS

A Great Group Project

The whole class can get in on the action to complete this large project. Enlarge a copy of the leaf pattern on page 81 onto heavy tagboard or poster board. Use a black marker to visually divide the leaf into a section for each student in the class. (If desired, make several patterns and divide the class into small groups to complete the project.) Provide a supply of markers, crayons, or paints and have each student decorate one section of the leaf. Display the finished project in the hallway or on an autumn bulletin board. Try adapting the project at different times during the year to create a turkey with fancy feathers, a festive Christmas tree, a colorful Valentine heart, and a brightly decorated Easter egg.

Snazzy Suncatchers

These colorful suncatchers will add sparkle to any classroom window. To make a suncatcher, each student will need the following materials: a supply of assorted tissue-paper pieces, plastic wrap, white glue, yarn, scissors, tape, a small piece of cardboard, and a paintbrush. Direct the student to tape a piece of plastic wrap to the cardboard, then paint an area of the plastic wrap with glue. Lay overlapping pieces of tissue paper over the glue; then paint another coat on top. Allow to dry overnight. Then peel the tissue paper away from the plastic wrap. Cut a shape from the tissue paper; then glue yarn around the shape. Add a yarn loop at the top of the shape, and then hang in a window. Watch the sunlight shine through with a rainbow of hues.

"Class-y" Collage

Create a unique display as students turn their names into works of art. Provide each student with a sheet of white construction paper on which his name is written in outlined letters as shown. Instruct each child to fill in the letters with brightly colored designs and drawings. When complete, have each student cut around his name. Arrange the resulting cutouts in a collage format on a piece of bulletin-board paper. Display the finished project on your classroom door for a "class-ic" decoration.

Joan Mary Macey, Benjamin Franklin School
Binghamton, NY

In Stitches

This project will have your class in stitches! Each student will need a pencil, a Styrofoam® meat tray, a large needle, and several lengths of thick thread in a variety of colors. Direct each student to lightly sketch a design on the tray with his pencil. Assist the student in threading the needle and tying a large knot at the end of the thread. Demonstrate how to stitch over the design by pushing the needle up through the underside of the tray and following the pencil sketch with stitches. Students may need to rethread the needle as different colors of thread are needed in the design. After the stitching is complete, show each student how to make a hanger by sewing a loop of thread to the top of the tray as shown. Hang the completed projects in the classroom for a display that is "sew" unique.

Doris Hautala, Washington Elementary, Ely, MN

Chalk Rubbings

By rubbing colored chalk over a set of stencils, your students will create a sunburst of color for your classroom. Provide each student with a cut-out set of the three apple patterns on page 82, a supply of colored chalk, several facial tissues, and a sheet of white construction paper. Instruct each student to use a different color of chalk to color each apple pattern. Starting with the smallest apple, the student places the pattern in the center of the construction paper and uses a tissue to rub the chalk from the pattern to the paper. Continue the process with the other apples, working from small to large. After each pattern has been rubbed onto the construction paper, have each student trim the paper leaving a border around the largest apple. Mount the colorful creations on a bulletin board for an eye-catching display.

Joan Mary Macey
Benjamin Franklin School
Binghamton, NY

Art By The Letter

Reinforce beginning sounds with this easy art project. Cut block letters from large pieces of oaktag or poster board. Give one letter to each student or pair of students. Instruct students to decorate the letters with drawings or magazine cutouts of pictures that begin with the letter. Mount the finished letters on construction paper, and use in a variety of phonics activities.

Get The Point?

Introduce the concept of *pointillism* as each student uses tiny dots of color to create a painting. Distribute a 9" x 12" piece of white construction paper to each student and instruct him to draw a simple design. Outline the shape with appropriate colors of markers. Using a cotton swab dipped in tempera paint, fill in the shape and background with points of color. When dry, mount each painting on a piece of black construction paper slightly larger than the painting itself. These works of art make a striking hallway exhibit or bulletin-board display.

Joan Mary Macey
Benjamin Franklin School
Binghamton, NY

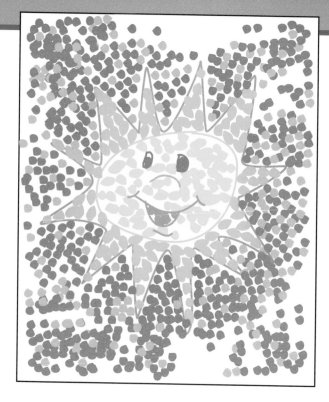

"Tee-rific" Art

This wearable art project can be enjoyed all year long! Send home a note requesting each parent to send a plain white T-shirt to school with his child. On a sheet of white drawing paper, each student uses a pencil to create a self-portrait or to draw a collection of items that represents his interests. Next he applies color to the paper with fabric crayons. Assist the student in transferring the design onto the T-shirt with an iron. Celebrate with a T-shirt day so that everyone can wear his shirt to school and show off his handiwork.

Marsha Carr-Lambert—Reading Specialist, West Side Elementary School, Cumberland, MD

Tissue-Paper Pictures

Brighten up your windows with these colorful works of art. Distribute a sheet of black construction paper to each child. Instruct her to fold the paper in half and cut out the center to create a frame. Cut a supply of various colors of tissue paper in different shapes and sizes. Apply glue to the edges of each piece of tissue paper and, one by one, glue them to each other by starting in a corner on the back of the frame. Completely fill the frame and set aside while the glue dries. Use the remainder of the black construction paper to cut a simple shape. When the glue has dried, turn the frame right-side up and affix the cutout to the tissue paper. Tape the finished project on a window and watch the sunlight catch the colors!

Fantastic Fish

This school of fish will make a big splash with your students! Provide each student with a 9" x 12" piece of white construction paper and a supply of markers. Instruct each student to use a pencil to sketch a fish shape on the paper. Next the student writes her name lightly in the fish shape, making sure that each letter extends from top to bottom (see example). Use markers to add color to the fish; then cut out the finished project. Arrange these exotic creatures on a bulletin board to create a "fin-tastic" display.

Joan Mary Macey
Benjamin Franklin School
Binghamton, NY

Crayon Batik

Batik, a textile craft, uses wax crayons to yield interesting results. Instruct each student to use bright crayons to draw and color a design on a piece of white art paper. Place the drawing in a pan of water for a few minutes. Remove the drawing and gently wad up the picture to create wrinkles in the paper. Flatten out the paper and place on dry newspaper. Paint over the drawing with one shade of watercolor; then quickly dip it back into the water. Place the paper back on the newspaper and allow it to dry. Mount the completed project on a piece of oaktag slightly larger than the drawing. The results? Beautiful batiks!

Bubble Prints

Printmaking is always an enjoyable activity—and this method lends itself to plenty of outdoor fun! Combine each of several colors of tempera paint with a small amount of liquid detergent into separate bowls. Direct students to use a straw to blow bubbles into the mixture until it rises to the rim. Place a 9" x 12" sheet of construction paper on top of the bowl to catch the imprint of the bubbles. Have students experiment with several colors of bubbles on each paper. The resulting print can be displayed as is, or used as a background for another art project.

A "Class-y" Collection Of Back-To-School Books

Enjoy this selection of back-to-school books for stories about new friends, new teachers, and comical classroom situations.

Lilly's Purple Plastic Purse
written by Kevin Henkes
Greenwillow Books

Lilly loves school—she loves her desk, her sharp pencils, and the chocolate milk in the lunchroom. She especially loves her teacher. But when Lilly brings her new purple plastic purse to school, she creates such a disturbance that her teacher has to take it away from her. Lilly reacts by doing something she later regrets, but she learns a good lesson about forgiveness.

Chrysanthemum
written by Kevin Henkes
Greenwillow Books

Chrysanthemum thinks she has the perfect name until she starts going to school, where the other children tease her. She starts to think that her name is dreadful! Fortunately, Chrysanthemum meets a teacher by the name of Mrs. Delphinium Twinkle, who reassures Chrysanthemum that she does indeed have a perfect name.

The Day The Teacher Went Bananas
written by James Howe and
illustrated by Lillian Hoban
E. P. Dutton

What happens when a mix-up sends a teacher to the zoo and a gorilla to school? Outrageous fun in the classroom! Students learn to count on their toes, swing from the trees, and monkey around with the art supplies. This story will have every student secretly wishing a gorilla would take over the classroom for a day.

Miss Malarkey Doesn't Live In Room 10

written by Judy Finchler and
illustrated by Kevin O'Malley
Walker Publishing Company, Inc.

What do teachers do after the students go home for the day? They make themselves at home. As the students imagine it, teachers have supper in the cafeteria, work out in the gym, and then go down the hall for a drink from the water fountain before going to sleep in the teacher's room. But when one teacher is spotted moving into an apartment building, the students have to readjust their thinking!

"Never Spit On Your Shoes"

written by Denys Cazet
Orchard Books

Arnie comes home from his first day of school with exciting stories about the many events of the day. From using brand-new crayons to eating lunch in the cafeteria, school was one big adventure. Students will enjoy Arnie's vivid descriptions as he tells about school as observed through the eyes of a first grader.

Emily At School

written by Suzanne Williams and
illustrated by Abby Carter
Hyperion Books for Children

The beginning of second grade brings new friends, new rules, and new adventures for Emily. Students will empathize with Emily's uncertainties about the routines in a new classroom, and rejoice as she takes on new challenges and makes the best of every situation.

Ruby The Copycat

written by Peggy Rathmann
Scholastic Inc.

On Ruby's first day of school, she makes friends with Angela, the pretty girl who sits right in front of her. The friendship is soon tested by Ruby's unrelenting copycat behavior. Thanks to an understanding teacher, the situation is handled in a way that allows Ruby and Angela to remain friends.

In Trouble With Teacher
written by Patricia Brennan Demuth and
illustrated by True Kelley
Dutton Children's Books
Third-grader Montgomery Thornton has always had trouble with spelling, and now it looks like he's about to fail his weekly spelling test. Although he promised himself he would study hard this week, something always interfered with study time. Montgomery spends the day dreading his teacher's angry reaction to his failing grade, until he discovers that teachers can be very caring people!

My Great-Aunt Arizona
written by Gloria Houston and
illustrated by Susan Condie Lamb
HarperCollins Publishers
Take students on a trip to the past, where a wooden schoolhouse held the lunch buckets, wood-burning stove, and high-button shoes of students long ago. Miss Arizona, the teacher in the one-room schoolhouse, taught the children of Henson Creek to read, write, and travel on the wings of a good book.

The Best Teacher In The World
written by Bernice Chardiet and Grace Maccarone
and illustrated by G. Brian Karas
Scholastic Inc.
Ms. Darcy is the nicest, prettiest, and smartest teacher in the whole world. When Bunny volunteers to deliver a note from Ms. Darcy, she is so excited to be chosen as a helper that she momentarily forgets that she has no idea where to take the note. Afraid to tell Ms. Darcy the truth, Bunny assures her that the note was safely delivered. After an anxious night, Bunny tells her teacher the truth, only to discover that Ms. Darcy is the most forgiving teacher in the world, too!

Spider School
written by Francesca Simon and
illustrated by Peta Coplans
Dial Books for Young Readers
Everything about the first day of school is going wrong for Kate—she has to wear tight shoes, she arrives late for class, and worst of all, there are no bathrooms at school! The day grows progressively worse, until Kate finds herself waking up from a bad dream. Fortunately, her *real* first day of school turns out to be much better.

My Teacher Sleeps In School
written by Leatie Weiss and
illustrated by Ellen Weiss
Viking Penguin Inc.

The students in Mrs. Marsh's class find a collection of clues that can lead to only one conclusion—their teacher sleeps in the classroom! From the pillow under her desk to the soap and towel in the closet, the students are convinced that Mrs. Marsh has made herself at home. When the students plan a bedtime surprise for their teacher, Mrs. Marsh treats them to an even bigger surprise!

Arthur's Teacher Trouble
written by Marc Brown
Little, Brown and Company

Homework on the first day of school, and a 100-word spelling test the first week! Arthur's third-grade teacher is the toughest teacher in the whole school. While other classes are popping popcorn and going on field trips, Mr. Ratburn's class is studying their spelling list. With hard work and encouragement from home, it looks like Arthur may be able to survive his teacher trouble.

How I Spent My Summer Vacation
written by Mark Teague
Crown Publishers, Inc.

It's Wallace's turn to tell how he spent his summer vacation, and what a vacation it was! Captured by cowboys, learning to rope and ride, and holding off an entire stampede—his story grows more fantastic by the minute. Just when you think nothing could top his adventure, Wallace announces that he can hardly wait for show-and-tell!

Open House

Open-House Video

Spend the week before Open House making a videotape of your students in action—scenes from the cafeteria, choral readings, musical performances, and recess activities. On the night of Open House, have the videotape playing in the back of your classroom for visitors to enjoy. The tape can be rewound and played throughout the evening. After Open House, the tape can be sent home with students whose parents were not able to attend the event. Parents will enjoy seeing their child in the routine of the school day.

Nancy Bauer—Gr. 2
Kidwell Elementary
Iowa Park, TX

Welcome!

Make the entryway to your classroom look inviting with this decorated welcome mat. Provide a sheet of poster board for students to decorate with colored markers. Have each student sign her name and add a small illustration. Laminate the finished product, then use masking tape to secure it to the floor in front of your doorway. Parents will feel as though you've rolled out the red carpet in their honor!

Sarah Mertz, Owenton, KY

Visitor's Guide

Enlist students' help in creating a visitor's guide that highlights points of interest in your classroom. Place students in small groups and assign each group a different area of the classroom to write about. Take photographs of each group working in the assigned area. Compile the completed writings and photos into a brochure and make a supply of photocopies to hand out at Open House. Keep a few extra copies on hand for new students and visitors who come during the school year. Visitors will feel right at home as they read about each area of your classroom.

Sarah Mertz
Owenton, KY

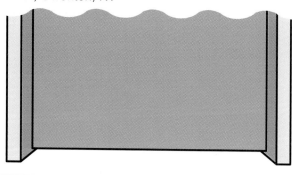

Top Ten

Create a display to welcome parents into your classroom by putting them on a top-ten list. Have each student compose a list of the top ten reasons he is glad his parent came to Open House. Post the lists on a bulletin board covered in red background paper and top them with musical notes made from the patterns on page 83. Add a black border and the title "Our Top Ten Lists." Parents will know you're glad to see them with so many reasons on display!

adapted from an idea by Doris Hautala
Washington Elementary
Ely, MN

Open-House Smiles

Take the opportunity at Open House to capture each student and his parents on film. Greet each visitor at the door with camera in hand, or ask a friend to be your photographer if you think you won't have time to snap the pictures yourself. When developing the film, request double prints. Send one copy of the photo home in a card with each student, thanking his parents for attending the event. Use the other copy for a poster-board display highlighting Open House activities. Mount the poster outside your classroom door for everyone to enjoy.

Sarah Mertz
Owenton, KY

Soothing Tunes

Create a relaxing mood in your classroom by playing soft music in the background during Open House. Choose a quiet, soothing melody, or make a recording of your students in music class. The background noise will help everyone feel more at ease and make your classroom feel like a comfortable, inviting place.

Sarah Mertz, Owenton, KY

Open-House Scavenger Hunt

Parents become detectives with this engaging Open-House activity. Make a list of the projects your students have completed and include them on a scavenger-hunt list. Add centers, bulletin boards, and other points of interest in the classroom to the list. Duplicate the list on colored paper and hand out a copy to each parent as he enters the room. Parents will be as excited as the students with this activity to lead them around the classroom.

Nicole Iacovazzi—Gr. 3
Owego Elementary
Vestal, NY

Scavenger Hunt

① Find the math center.

② Look at the dinosaur display.

③ Visit the library corner.

Sweet Surprise

Entice visitors into your classroom with a platter of student-made cookies for Open House. Use a basic sugar-cookie recipe or a package of refrigerated cookie dough and several apple-shaped cookie cutters. If desired, tint the dough with red food coloring ahead of time. Have students roll out the dough, cut out the shapes, and place the cookies on baking sheets. Ask for parent volunteers to supervise the baking. Students will be proud to serve these tasty treats to their parents as they pay a visit to the classroom during Open House.

Sarah Mertz
Owenton, KY

The Estimation Station

Parents will get a chance to be students again with this Open-House activity. Fill a jar with assorted goodies and decorate the lid with bows and ribbons. Place an empty box and slips of paper next to the jar. At Open House, tell parents to estimate with their child the number of treats in the jar. Instruct them to write their names and estimate on a slip of paper to be placed in the box. If desired, request additional information about the estimate, asking if it is an odd or even number; how many tens and ones are in the estimate; or to round the number to the nearest ten. Count the goodies with your students the next day. Read each estimate aloud to determine the closest guess. Send the jar home with the winning student to share with his family.

Nicole Iacovazzi—Gr. 3
Owego Elementary
Vestal, NY

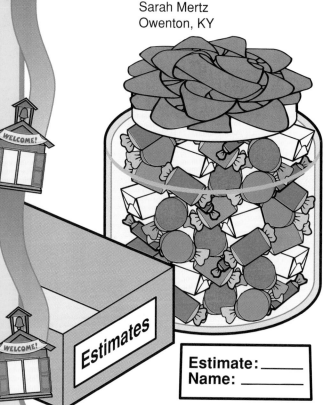

Estimates

Estimate:_____
Name: _____

Parent Portraits

Open House commonly includes pictures that students have drawn of themselves. For this Open House, why not let students draw pictures of the visitors who plan to attend Open House with them? Encourage each student to create a likeness of his parents wearing work uniforms, performing daily tasks, or participating in a favorite activity. These drawings can be placed on students' desks or arranged on a bulletin-board display along with the title, "Look Who's Coming To Open House!" Parents will enjoy seeing themselves through this kid's-eye view!

Nancy Bauer—Gr. 2
Kidwell Elementary
Iowa Park, TX

Delightful Desk Markers

Parents will be able to quickly locate their child's desk when you use these cute cutouts as desk markers. Use the patterns on page 84 for students to trace onto the folds of manila folders. Cut out each figure on the fold so the resulting figure will stand up. Use student photos to paste on the faces of corresponding girl or boy figures; then have each student color the rest of her cutout in her own likeness. Stand each child's completed figure on her desk. What a fun way for parents to find their child's place in the classroom, and a great keepsake to take home with them, too!

Joan Costello—Gr. 1, William McGinn School, Scotch Plains, NJ

Hosts And Hostesses

Give your students the opportunity to host Open House in your classroom. Discuss ideas for showing parents the classroom centers, bulletin boards, and other displays. Remind students that they should remain with their parents during the tour of the room, and to take their parents to see the library, cafeteria, and other important places on the school grounds. Parents will see the enthusiasm their children have for school, and you are left to greet parents and answer questions.

Susan Wilson—Gr. 1
Sevierville Elementary
Sevierville, TN

A Colorful Event

Brighten your classroom with bursts of color as you prepare for Open House with this captivating crayon theme. Use the following ideas for decorating your room with splashes of color and creative student-made projects.

A Colorful Class

Begin preparations for the big night by having students assist in creating a classroom bulletin-board display titled "A Colorful Class Of Kids." Use the pattern on page 85 to duplicate a class set of crayon patterns on colored copy paper. Instruct each student to cut out a crayon. Attach a photo of the student in the circle on the crayon wrapper. Challenge each student to create a color name for the crayon using her name as part of the title (see example). Arrange the colorful creations on a bulletin board for parents to enjoy.

Bright Barbara

Spectacular Sculptures

Surround the scene with more color as students use enlarged copies of the pattern on page 85 to fashion soft-sculpture crayons. Direct each student to write her name in the center of two crayon patterns, then fill them in using her favorite color. Cut out each pattern and glue them together, color-side out, leaving an opening at the base of the crayon. Stuff the shape with crumpled tissue or newspaper and glue the base together. Punch a small hole in the figure and thread a length of yarn through the opening. Suspend the spectacular sculptures from the ceiling for a rainbow of color.

Haley

Magnetic Moments

Have a token of appreciation ready to give visitors as they tour your classroom during Open House. Purchase a crayon-shaped rubber stamp and a supply of magnetic sticker paper (available at craft stores). Use the stamp to create crayon shapes on the magnetic paper. Have students cut out the shapes and color them with a variety of permanent markers. Attach the resulting magnets to a chalkboard or filing cabinet and distribute to parents as take-home gifts. Invite parents to use the magnets to attach spelling lists, important notes, and student artwork to their refrigerators at home.

Rainbow Of Refreshments

Dish out a rainbow of refreshments by distributing bowls of brightly wrapped fruit-flavored candy and candy-coated chocolate pieces throughout the room. If desired, prepare powdered drink mix in a variety of colors and serve in clear glasses. The vivid assortment will convince parents that your class is indeed a colorful bunch of kids!

adapted from ideas by Julie Plowman—Gr. 3
Adair-Casey Elementary, Adair, IA

An "A-peel-ing" Open House

Set the tone for your Open House night with a bushel of ideas to welcome parents into your classroom.

Shimmering Apples

Decorate your room with a sparkling display of shiny apples. Pour a mixture of equal parts salt and red powdered tempera paint into an empty saltshaker. Prepare containers of yellow- and green-tinted salt in the same manner. Distribute a tagboard apple cutout (see patterns on page 82) to each student and instruct him to use a paintbrush to coat it with a layer of watered-down glue. Sprinkle tinted salt over the glue and allow to dry. Shake off any excess salt; then repeat the procedure to coat the other side of the apple. Suspend these fantastic fruits from the ceiling.

Please Come!

Extend a special invitation for parents to attend Open House with apple-print notes. Provide each student with an apple that has been cut in half. Have students dip their apple halves into red tempera paint, then create a print on a square of white construction paper. If desired, have students use markers to draw stems and leaves on their apple prints. Write the date and time of the Open House on the board for students to copy onto their invitations. Send the notes home a day or two before the event to encourage a terrific turnout.

"Tree-mendous" Work

Show parents what good apples your students are with a bumper crop of bragging! Fashion an apple tree from green and brown bulletin-board paper. Mount the tree on a wall or door in your classroom. Then use the patterns on page 82 to duplicate a class supply of apples on red or yellow copy paper. Write the name of each student on an apple along with a positive comment about the student. Decorate the tree with the comments of praise for your students.

An Apple A Day

Serve up a tasty treat to visitors and parents with some "apple-tizing" refreshments. Provide a variety of yellow, red, and green apple slices and a bowl of fruit or caramel dip for parents to munch as they tour your classroom. For drinks, serve apple juice, of course!

Birthdays & Celebrations

Don't Forget!

Students with summer birthdays seem to always miss out on the birthday fun. Not anymore! Set aside time during the first and the last few weeks of school to honor these special students. If a student's birthday falls near the later half of the summer, celebrate his birthday on a day during the first few weeks of school. If the student's birthday falls in the first half of the summer, celebrate his birthday on a day during the last few weeks of school. Now *all* your students will be able to have the thrill of being the birthday child for the day!

Jan Masengale—Gr. 1
New Castle, IN

A Birthday Banner

Save time and energy by making a birthday banner that will last throughout the school year. Use a computer to print a banner labeled "Happy Birthday!" Then ask each child to sign his name and birth date. Invite students to work in small groups to decorate the banner with birthday designs such as gift-wrapped presents, confetti, and party hats. Display the completed banner on a classroom wall for all to see. Now that's an easy-to-make birthday decoration that everyone will love!

Rita Petrocco—Gr. 1

Birthday Reminders

Never forget another student's birthday with this idea for birthday flash cards. Print each student's name and birthday on the blank side of a 3" x 5" flash card. (Be sure to make a flash card for yourself, too!) Stack the completed flash cards in order beginning with the birthdays during the first month of school; then display the flash cards in an area of the classroom where they can easily be seen. After each student celebrates his birthday, place his flash card behind the other cards. With just a quick glance, you can see which student will be celebrating the next birthday. These flash cards are also great for graphing students' birthdays by months.

Rita Petrocco—Gr. 1
Holy Cross School
Nepean, Ontario
Canada

Guess Who?

Here's an idea for making a birthday-riddle bulletin board that is guaranteed to fill your classroom with laughter! In advance ask each child to bring in a baby photograph of herself. Provide each child with an 8 1/2" x 11" piece of paper. Instruct each child to fold her paper in half and tape her photograph to the top of the front cover. Next have her write a birthday riddle describing herself and the date of her birthday under the photograph. Then ask the child to write her name on the inside of her booklet. Display the completed riddles on a bulletin board covered with birthday wrapping paper and add the title, "Guess Who?" Let the laughter begin!

Rita Petrocco—Gr. 1
Holy Cross School
Nepean, Ontario
Canada

I have brown hair and blue eyes. I love to rollerblade. My birthday is January 1. Who am I?

Measuring Up Birthdays

Cook up some practice with measurement skills with this tasty birthday idea. At the end of each month, enlist students' help in preparing a class supply of cupcakes, a class birthday cake, or homemade ice cream to honor students with recent birthdays. To prepare the treat, divide the class into several small groups. Invite each group to assist you in a different stage of preparing the dessert. Before students dig into the tasty treat, lead them in a round of "Happy Birthday To You!" to celebrate the honorees' birthdays.

Rita Petrocco—Gr. 1

Birthday Cupcakes

Enlist your youngsters' help in creating this calendar sequencing center and display. On white construction paper, duplicate student copies of the cupcake patterns on page 86. After each youngster has colored a cupcake, label his project with his name and birth date. Laminate and cut out the shapes; then use a permanent marker to program the backs of the cutouts for self-checking. Store the cutouts in a birthday gift bag at a center. A student arranges the cutouts in sequential order; then he flips the cutouts to check his work. After each child has completed the center activity, display the cutouts in sequential order across a classroom wall. With just a quick glance, students can easily see the dates of their classmates' birthdays!

Rita Petrocco—Gr. 1

Birthday Murals

Invite students to discover the exciting events that occur near their birthdays with this fun-filled tip. Divide students into four groups based on the season in which their birthdays occur. Supply each group with a large piece of bulletin-board paper and several markers. Instruct each group to brainstorm events that take place during their season and then draw pictures describing the events. Display the completed murals on a classroom wall.

Ideas By Rita Petrocco—Gr. 1
Holy Cross School
Nepean, Ontario, Canada

Birthdays Are "Write" On!

Add creative writing to student birthdays with this unique idea. While students are making cards for the birthday child, ask the birthday child to do some creative writing. Consider story starters such as "The Year Everyone Forgot My Birthday," "The Birthday Surprise," "The Unwrapped Present," or "Wasn't That A Party!" After the special student completes the story, invite her to share her story with the class. Then have her classmates present the birthday cards to her along with their best rendition of "Happy Birthday To You!"

Rita Petrocco—Gr. 1

Penny Cake

Heads or tails? It doesn't matter which side of the penny you get in this party idea. In advance place a foil-wrapped penny in cake batter; then bake and decorate the cake. Cut the cake into the same number of slices as you have students. At the end of the classroom celebration, invite each student to take a piece of cake. Instruct students to be on the lookout for the foil-wrapped penny as they eat their pieces of cake. Provide a special treat to the student who gets the piece of cake with the penny in it. What an exciting finish to any classroom celebration!

Sarah Mertz
Owenton, KY

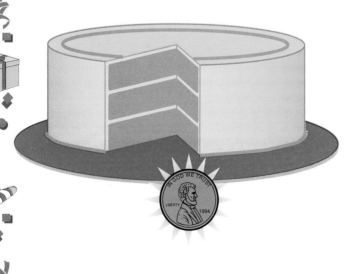

Time To Celebrate!

Add excitement to birthday celebrations with this timely activity. A week prior to each child's birthday, send home a note asking parents to help their child make a timeline of his life. Instruct the student to start with the day he was born and continue to the current year. Encourage the child to focus on a specific area of his life, such as vacations or birthdays. Invite each child to share his timeline on his birthday. Not only are your youngsters gaining a better concept of time, they're discovering the uniquenesses of their classmates, too!

Mary Jo Kampschnieder
Howells Community Catholic Schools
Howells, NE

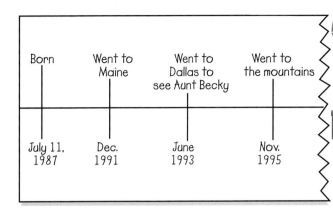

Born	Went to Maine	Went to Dallas to see Aunt Becky	Went to the mountains
July 11, 1987	Dec. 1991	June 1993	Nov. 1995

B-I-R-T-H-D-A-Y-S

Hold the cake! Birthdays aren't just for celebrating anymore—they can be used to teach language arts skills, too! On each child's birthday, use the word *birthdays* to teach a different skill. Consider skills such as compound words, two-syllable words, words that begin with the letter *b*, plural words, words with *th*, and words with *ay*. Students are sure to find these lessons more exciting when a favorite event is the focus of the lesson!

Rita Petrocco—Gr. 1, Holy Cross School, Nepean, Ontario, Canada

Piñata Pleasures

Add flair to any celebration by making piñatas! To make piñatas, blow up a large balloon for each child and provide students with strips of newspaper. Instruct each child to cover his balloon with strips dipped into wheat paste. After the newspaper has dried overnight, have students decorate their piñatas to match the current theme. Consider providing art materials such as colored tissue paper, construction paper, felt, yarn, and paint. When this has dried, cut a small hole in the back of each piñata and have the student insert individually wrapped treats. To complete the projects, attach a string to the top of each piñata. Invite students to take their piñatas home to break and share with their families. Now that's a fiesta of fun! Olé!

Sarah Mertz
Owenton, KY

57

Games

Puzzle Storage

Puzzles are the perfect activity for indoor recess or quiet center games, but after several uses, the boxes become worn. Solve this problem with an organized storage system. Cut the picture from the top of the puzzle box and store it along with the puzzle pieces in a clear plastic storage box. The picture can still be used as a reference when assembling the puzzle, and the durability of the container will help it last for years to come. To further organize your puzzles, number each box and copy the number on the back of each puzzle piece stored in the box. When stray pieces turn up, you'll know exactly where each piece belongs.

Beth Mohon—Grs. 2–3
Drakesboro Elementary
Drakesboro, KY

What Game Will Be Next?

7-up

Group Game Spinner

Create a democratic way to decide which group game your class will play with this game-selecting spinner. Ask the class to brainstorm the various games you play as a class. When the list is complete, write the name of each game on a pie-shaped wedge on a paper plate. Cut a pie-shaped wedge from a second paper plate and place the plate on top of the first one, so that the name of one game is exposed. Secure the plates with a brad through the center. Display the completed spinner on a corner of the chalkboard. When the opportunity for a game arises, the class will play the game featured in the open wedge. Afterward the spinner is turned one space clockwise, showing the name of the next game to be played. With the spinner to announce the name of the game, it's one less decision you'll have to make!

Renae Little—Substitute Teacher
Lilburn, GA

Bingo With A Twist

Use an ordinary set of bingo cards for a game that focuses on reinforcing basic math facts. Distribute a card to each student and play the game according to the traditional rules, with the exception of calling out the numbers. Instead of announcing a letter and number, call out a math fact equal to the number selected. For example, for "G, 50," call out "G, 40 + 10." Allow time for students to solve the equation and look for the answer on their cards. Your students will be eager to find the sums and differences when they consider math practice to be fun and games!

Kay Smith
St. Charles Borromeo
Bloomington, IN

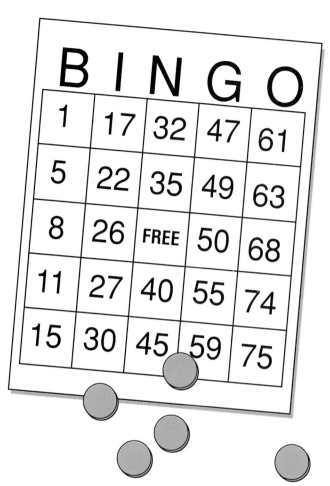

Catch A Question

Liven up a lesson with the use of a beanbag or foam football. When it's time for a lesson review, have the beanbag in hand as you ask a question. If a student wants to volunteer an answer, she raises her hand and you toss her the beanbag. The student catches the beanbag, answers the question, then tosses it back to you. Watch student participation soar to new heights when the children are motivated with a simple game of catch.

Lori Sammartino
Clayton Traditional Academy
Pittsburgh, PA

Come On Out!

This game is great for becoming acquainted with new classmates, or just fun to play on a rainy day when outdoor recess isn't possible. To play, select a student to be "It" and have her go out in the hallway where she can't view the class. While the student is out of the room, choose another student to hide behind your desk as the rest of the class changes seats. When everyone is situated, call the first student in from the hallway and ask her to identify the student who is hiding. Since all students have switched seats, the empty desk may not belong to the student who is hiding, making the game a little more difficult. After the player who is "It" has made her guess, the class choruses, "Come on out!" to the student in hiding. Play continues as the student in hiding becomes the new "It." Students will love being able to get up and move even when the weather is too dreary for outdoor games.

Beth Mohon—Grs. 2–3
Drakesboro Elementary
Drakesboro, KY

Hot-Potato Review

Have a sizzling review session for any subject with a game of Hot Potato. Stuff an old pantyhose leg with cotton batting and stitch the opening closed to create a giant spud. Have students sit in a circle and pass the potato as you play a musical recording. When the music stops, the student holding the potato must answer a review question. If he answers correctly, he gets to sit in the hot seat (the center of the circle) until someone else qualifies to take his place. This game will be a red-hot favorite with students all year long!

Beanbag Grammar

Toss around the parts of speech for a great grammar review. Arrange your class in a circle and hand a beanbag to one student. The student names a part of speech, such as "noun" or "verb," then tosses the beanbag to another student. The second student must catch the beanbag and say a word that falls in the category named by the first student. If he is correct, play continues. If he is incorrect, prompt him to help him remember the definition of that part of speech; then give him another opportunity to say a word. The beanbag is tossed around the circle until each student has had a turn to say a word for the designated part of speech. Grammar review will soon be a favorite activity!

adapted from an idea by Malinda Borum
Glenwood Elementary School
Virginia Beach, VA

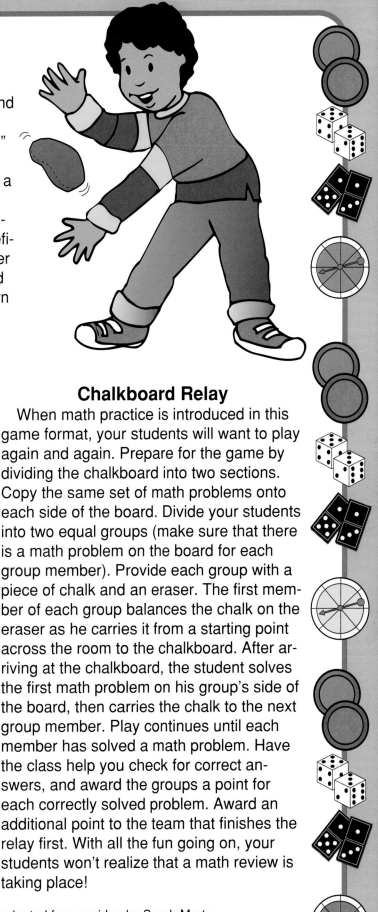

Chalkboard Relay

When math practice is introduced in this game format, your students will want to play again and again. Prepare for the game by dividing the chalkboard into two sections. Copy the same set of math problems onto each side of the board. Divide your students into two equal groups (make sure that there is a math problem on the board for each group member). Provide each group with a piece of chalk and an eraser. The first member of each group balances the chalk on the eraser as he carries it from a starting point across the room to the chalkboard. After arriving at the chalkboard, the student solves the first math problem on his group's side of the board, then carries the chalk to the next group member. Play continues until each member has solved a math problem. Have the class help you check for correct answers, and award the groups a point for each correctly solved problem. Award an additional point to the team that finishes the relay first. With all the fun going on, your students won't realize that a math review is taking place!

adapted from an idea by Sarah Mertz
Owenton, KY

Bulletin Boards

This Way To Your New Room

Show new students the way to your room with a poster-board street sign to point them in the right direction. Draw and color the desired shape on the poster board and cut out the resulting sign. Add your name, grade level, and room number. Place the sign atop a pole made from cardboard wrapping-paper tubes covered in butcher paper. Set the sign outside your classroom door, and your students will find their destination with no trouble at all.

VaReane Heese, Springfield Elementary
Omaha, NE

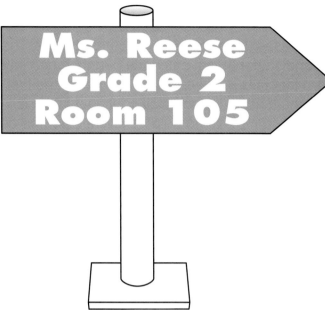

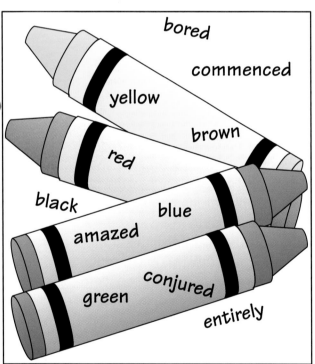

Theme Displays

Capture the magic of each theme you teach during the school year with poster displays of key vocabulary, facts, and ideas. For each new theme or unit you introduce, prepare a poster with a simple drawing that represents the topic. Laminate the poster and place it in a central part of your classroom. Each time a new vocabulary word or fact is introduced, write it on the poster. At the end of the unit, keep the poster on display in the classroom. Continue to make posters for each new theme, keeping both old and new topics on display. By the end of the year, your room will be filled with all the learning that has taken place.

Susan Wilson—Gr. 1, Sevierville Elementary
Sevierville, TN

Clip It!

Showing off students' work will be a snap (or a clip!) with this alternative to the traditional bulletin-board display. Prepare your classroom for an instant exhibit by suspending spring-type clothespins from your ceiling with monofilament line. Simply clip student artwork, seasonal decorations, or visual aids to the clothespins and your display is complete. And without staples or thumbtacks to deal with, taking down the display is just as easy!

Kathleen N. Kopp, Lecanto Primary School, Lecanto, FL

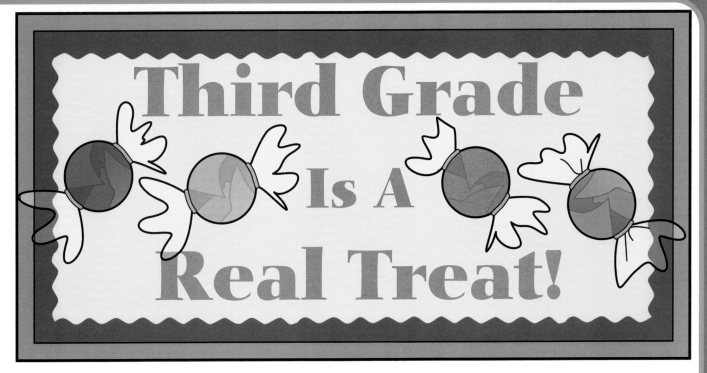

Let students know what a treat a new school year can be! Create this tempting display with an assortment of colored tissue paper and a roll of clear cellophane. Wrap a piece of cellophane around a sheet of crumpled tissue paper to resemble a wrapped candy. Secure the ends of the cellophane with rubber bands. Make several candies and pin them to the board in a mouthwatering array. Add the title, a colorful border, and you're off to a sweet start!

Sarah Moseley—Teacher Aide, Mertzon, TX

Each student will put her best foot forward to create this beginning-of-the-year display. Instruct each student to trace her right foot on a piece of tagboard and cut out the resulting shape. Have the student write her name and draw a face on the cutout. Mount the completed characters on the board and add the title, "We're Starting Out On The Right Foot!" Now that's a "toe-riffic" display!

Kathleen N. Kopp, Lecanto Primary School, Lecanto, FL

This tail-waggin' task board will have your pups eager to perform classroom duties. Enlarge several copies of the bone pattern on page 87. Program each bone with a classroom job title and arrange on a bulletin board. Duplicate a class supply of puppy patterns from page 87 and have each student color, cut out, and write his name on a pattern. Assign a classroom duty by pinning a puppy cutout under a job title. Add the title and you'll be ready for some helpful hounds.

Kathleen N. Kopp, Lecanto Primary School, Lecanto, FL

Equip your students for classroom tasks with this job-assignment display. Enlarge several copies of the toolbox pattern on page 88. Laminate each toolbox before writing the title of a classroom job on it; then mount it on the board. Duplicate a copy of the hammer pattern on page 88 for each student. Have the student write his name on a hammer before coloring it and cutting it out. Assign classroom duties by pinning a hammer by a toolbox. As the title proclaims, you'll have some hardworking helpers!

Kathleen N. Kopp, Lecanto Primary School, Lecanto, FL

For an unusual way to create a birthday display, don't keep this idea under wraps! Use a variety of gift wrap to cut 12 rectangular shapes. Use a marker to write the name of one month of the year on each rectangle, then mount on a bulletin board. Top each rectangle with a bow. Attach a gift tag bearing a student's name to the package with his corresponding birthday month. Complete the display with the title, "Happy Birthday To You!"

Rita Petrocco—Gr. 1, Holy Cross School, Nepean, Ontario, Canada

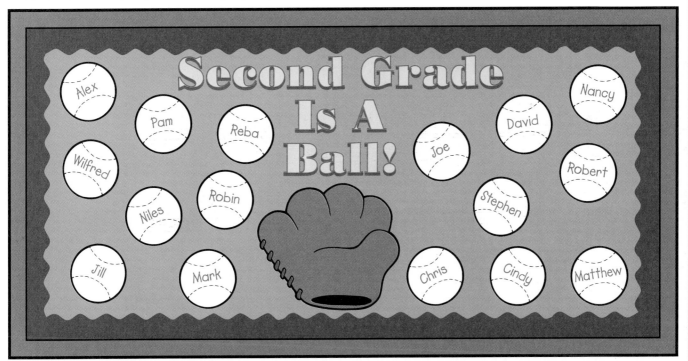

Create team spirit with this welcome-back bulletin board. Enlarge the baseball-glove pattern on page 89 and mount in the center of your bulletin board. Duplicate a class supply of baseball shapes from the pattern on page 89 and program each with the name of a student. Arrange the cutouts around the baseball glove and add the title using the appropriate grade level. You're sure to set the stage for a winning team!

Nancy Bauer—Gr. 2, Kidwell Elementary, Iowa Park, TX

Greet students with a glittering display to welcome them back to school. Cover a bulletin board with black background paper and trim with a gold border. Add a cluster of enticing awards such as a golden honor-roll certificate, an Olympic medal–style reading award, a shimmering perfect-attendance recognition, and a shiny "Spelling Star" certificate. Add the title using letters fashioned from gold wrapping paper to complete the brilliant display.

Debbie Witte—Gr. 2, Roger E. Sides Elementary, Karnes City, TX

This hands-on activity will produce a birthday bulletin board that can stay on display all year long. Enlarge the pattern on page 90 to make a set of cakes labeled with each month of the year. Arrange the cakes in chronological order on a bulletin board. Duplicate a class supply of candles using the patterns on page 90 and distribute one to each student. The student writes his name and birthdate on the candle, then places it on the cake that corresponds with his birth month.

Kelly A. Wong—Gr. 2, Berlyn School, Ontario, CA

Encourage students to share some summer reading with this rootin'-tootin' display. Enlarge and color the cowboy pattern on page 91 and mount it on the board. If desired, attach a real bandanna to the cowboy. Add a display of book reports students have written about their summer reading. Corral the reports with a lasso made from twine. Add the title, and you're set for a reading roundup!

Nicole Iacovazzi—Gr. 3, Owego Elementary, Vestal, NY

"Ant-icipate" the first day of school with this message to welcome your new students. Cover a bulletin board with a red-and-white-checked tablecloth. Using the patterns on page 92, duplicate and color an ant for each student in your class. Program the ants with the names of your students before arranging them along the border. Complete the display by adding the title and several 6-inch paper plates with subject names printed on them. Your class will know that the coming year will be a real picnic!

Ann Moseley, Irion County Elementary, Mertzon, TX

Send a "bunch" of greetings with this welcoming bulletin-board display. Cut a 4-inch circle from purple construction paper for each student in your class. Label each circle with a student's name, and arrange on a bulletin board as shown. Attach a brown construction-paper stem to the top of the arrangement. Before adding the title, create a border with an artificial vine.

Julie Eick-Granchelli, Towne Elementary, Medina, NY

These hot-air balloons will get you off to a high-flying new school year. Enlarge the pattern on page 93 to create several hot-air balloons. Program each balloon with a theme or topic of study for the upcoming year. Mount the balloons on a blue background and add several cloud cutouts. Write the title across the cloud shapes, and your class will be prepared for liftoff!

Amy Anderson—Gr. 3, All Saints Episcopal, Tyler, TX

Watch the pieces of a new year fall into place with this interactive bulletin-board activity. Prior to the first day of school, visually divide a sheet of poster board into puzzle-piece sections—one section for each student in the class. Outline each section in black marker; then cut apart the pieces. Distribute a section to each student on the first day of school. Instruct the student to write his name and draw a picture of himself on the puzzle piece. When everyone is finished, assemble the puzzle and mount it on a bulletin board. Add a border and title, and the puzzle becomes a class display.

Julie Eick-Granchelli, Towne Elementary, Medina, NY

Part of the excitement of a new school year is buying school supplies and selecting a new lunchbox. Capitalize on the excitement by using a lunchbox as a bulletin-board design. Duplicate a class set of the lunchbox pattern on page 94. Distribute a copy to each student and have her create a design featuring her likeness. Mount the completed projects on a bulletin board; then add a border and the title. See you in the lunch line!

Amy Anderson—Gr. 3, All Saints Episcopal, Tyler, TX

This student-made bulletin-board idea is a great project for the first day of school. Cover a bulletin board with blue background paper. Distribute a piece of yellow construction paper to each student and instruct him to trace around his hand. Cut out the resulting shape and have each student write his name on his cutout. Staple the cutouts in a circle on the bulletin board. Add the title in the center of the display, and your class-created board is complete.

Rita Petrocco—Gr. 1, Holy Cross School
Nepean, Ontario, Canada

Welcome students to hop into a new school year with a display of jumping joeys. Duplicate a copy of the kangaroo and pennant patterns on page 95 for each student. Write each student's name on a pennant before attaching the figures to the board as shown. Add a border and the title to complete the display.

Beverly Langland, Trinity Christian Academy, Jacksonville, FL

Add southwestern flavor to your back-to-school bulletin board with this tasty display. To create the board you will need a straw bread basket cut in half, a red bandanna, a sheet of oaktag, and a package of yellow or orange crinkled gift-wrap stuffing. Arrange the bandanna in the basket half and mount on a bulletin board covered with green background paper. Cut the oaktag into a class supply of triangle shapes, and lightly color with yellow and brown crayons to resemble tortilla chips. Write the name of each student on a chip and place it in the basket. "Drizzle" on a layer of "cheese" using the crinkled gift-wrap stuffing, add the title and a festive border, and your display will look good enough to eat!

Sarah Moseley—Teacher Aide, Mertzon, TX

This undersea bulletin board is guaranteed to make a big splash with students! Use the patterns on page 96 to create a class supply of ocean creatures. Color the patterns, cut them out, and label each with a student's name. If desired, glue a wiggle eye to each cutout, then mount on a bulletin board covered with blue background paper. Add a border and the title, and you'll be in the swim for a new year.

adapted from an idea by Debbie Witte—Gr. 2, Roger E. Sides Elementary, Karnes City, TX

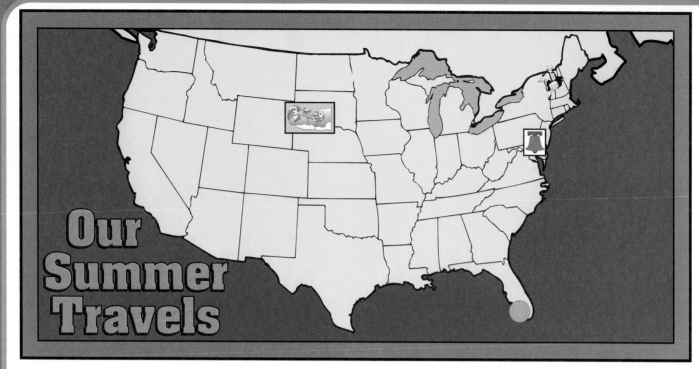

Our Summer Travels

This bulletin-board display lends itself to an instant geography lesson! Obtain a large map of the United States and Canada and mount it on your bulletin board. During the first week of school, ask students to bring in postcards or photographs of places they visited over the summer. Attach the pictures to the corresponding places on the map. Students will have a visual aid to compare distances traveled, directions of their journeys, and common areas of travel.

Joan Mary Macey, Benjamin Franklin School, Binghamton, NY

Be famous in your school for this eye-catching display! Ask students to gather a few of their favorite photos from home. Provide each student with a sheet of poster board and instruct him to decorate it with photos and captions. If desired, students may add illustrations or small items to complement the photographs. Display the completed posters in a hallway with the title "Our Wall Of Fame."

Nicole Iacovazzi—Gr. 3, Owego Elementary, Vestal, NY

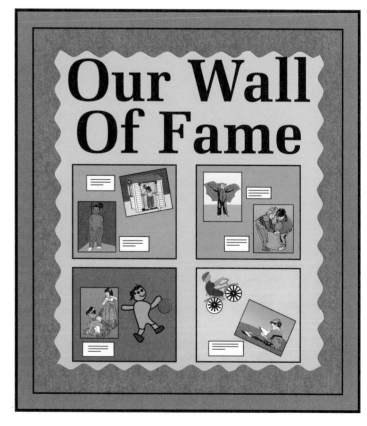

Our Wall Of Fame

Patterns
Use with "Coming Attractions" on page 4.

ADMIT ONE
Great Student Into
The Classroom

signed _____

WELCOME!

©1997 The Education Center, Inc. • *BACK-TO-SCHOOL BOOK* • *Primary* • TEC1120

COMING ATTRACTIONS ★

★ In the next few weeks we will learn about:

★ _____

★ _____

★ _____

★ _____

And you will have a starring role! ★

©1997 The Education Center, Inc. • *BACK-TO-SCHOOL BOOK* • *Primary* • TEC1120

NAME BINGO

		FREE SPACE		

Note To The Teacher: Use With "Name Bingo" on page 22.

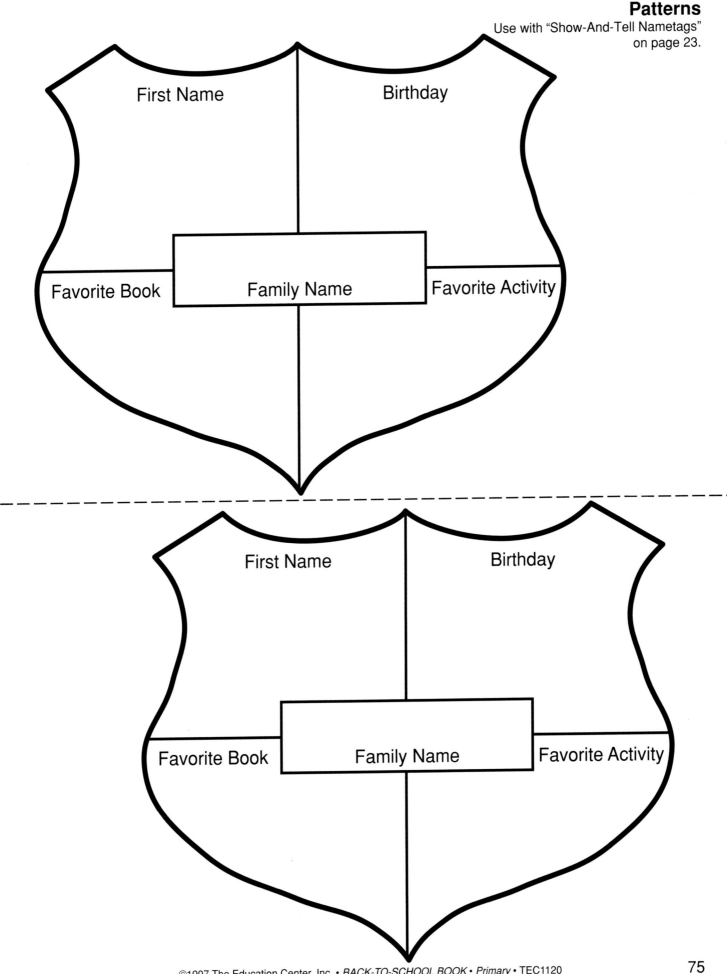

First Name

Birthday

Favorite Book

Family Name

Favorite Activity

First Name

Birthday

Favorite Book

Family Name

Favorite Activity

CLASSROOM TIMES

Teacher: _____ Date: _____

Events

Reminders

Superstars

Special Thanks

Help Wanted

Note To The Teacher: Use with "In The News" on page 31.

Sunday	Monday	Tuesday	Wednesday	Thursday	Friday	Saturday

Note To The Teacher: Use with "Reading Calendar" on page 32 and "Weekly Behavior Log" on page 37.

Awards

Use with "Proud As A Peacock" on page 33.

Proud As A Peacock!

We are very proud of _____

because _____

_____

_____

Date: _____

Signed: _____

Proud As A Peacock!

We are very proud of _____

because _____

_____

_____

Date: _____

Signed: _____

Dear Parent,

Your child is very special! Please use this form to share any important information, special goals, or medical concerns about your child.

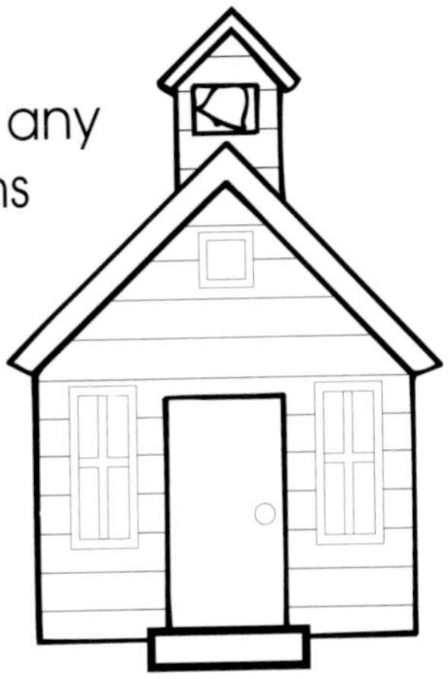

Student: ______________________________

Remarks: ______________________________

____

____

____

____

____

Dear Parent,

Your child is very special! Please use this form to share any important information, special goals, or medical concerns about your child.

Student: ______________________________

Remarks: ______________________________

____

____

____

____

____

©1997 The Education Center, Inc. • *BACK-TO-SCHOOL BOOK* • *Primary* • TEC1120

Note To The Teacher: Use with "Getting Acquainted" on page 35.

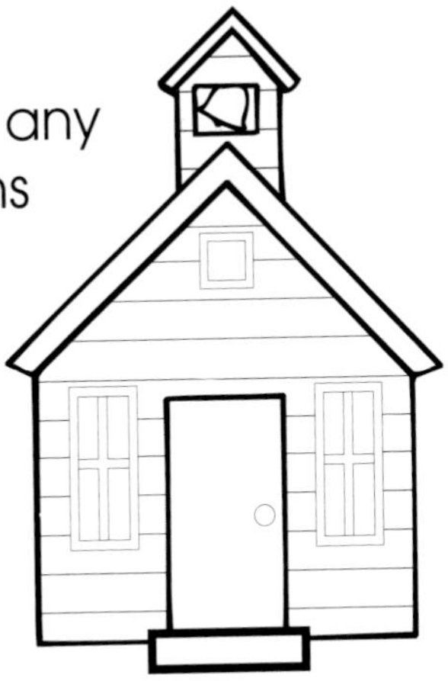

Patterns
Use with "Keys To A Good Year" on page 36.

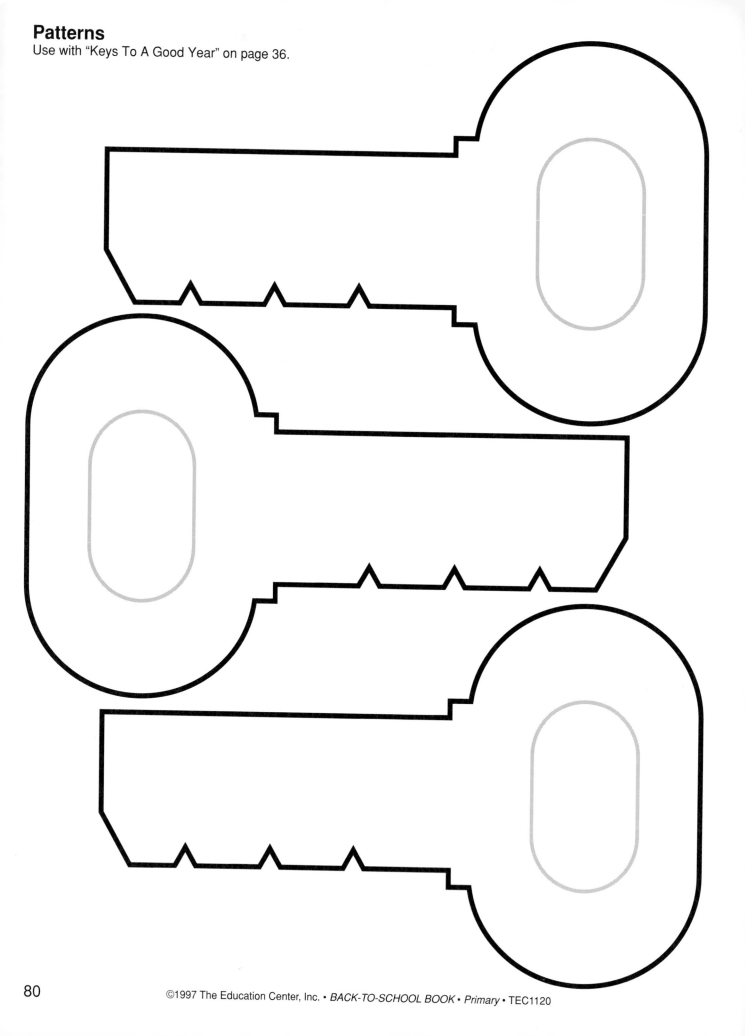

You're The
Apple Of
My Eye!

_____
name

Keep Up The
Good Work!

©1997 The Education
Center, Inc.

©1997 The Education Center, Inc. • *BACK-TO-SCHOOL BOOK* • *Primary* • TEC1120

Pattern
Use with "A Great Group Project" on page 40.

Patterns

Use with "Chalk Rubbings" on page 41, and "Shimmering Apples" and
" 'Tree-mendous' Work" on page 53.

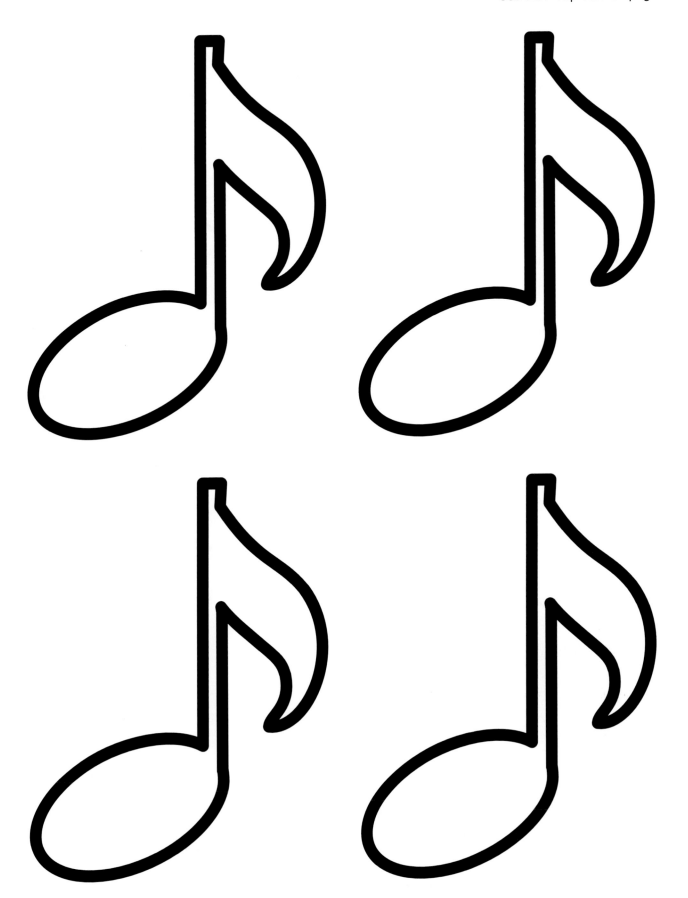

Patterns

Use with "Delightful Desk Markers" on page 51.

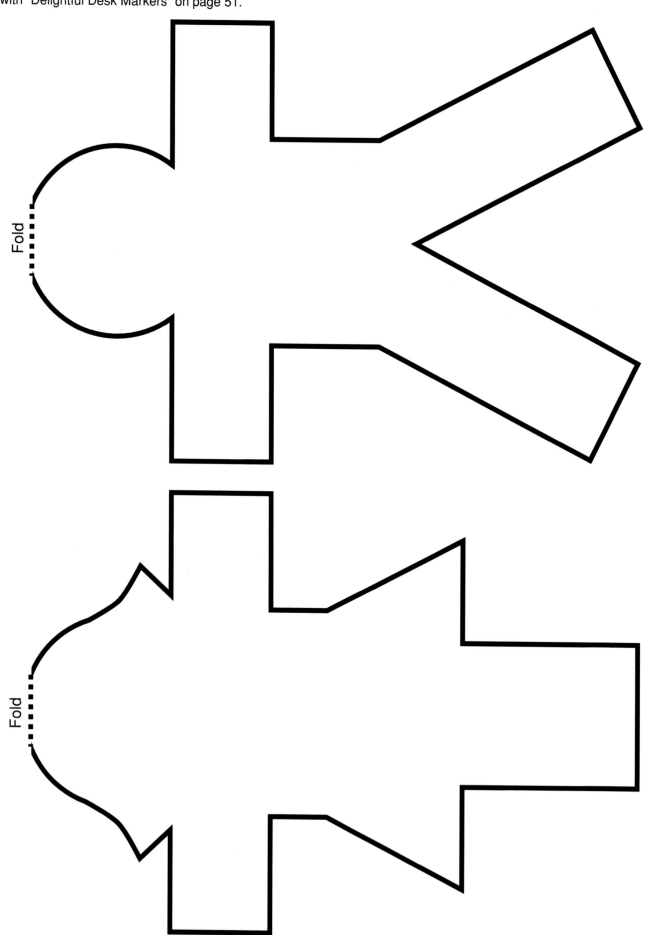

Fold

Fold

©1997 The Education Center, Inc. • *BACK-TO-SCHOOL BOOK* • *Primary* • TEC1120

Patterns

Use with "Birthday Cupcakes" on page 55.

Паттернс

Patterns

Use with "Hardworking Helpers" on page 64.

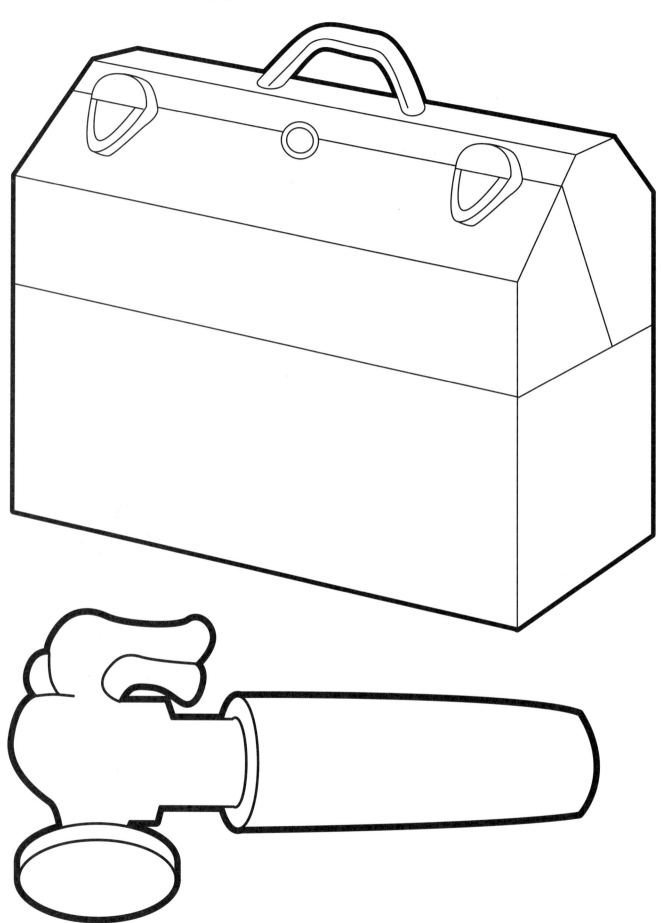

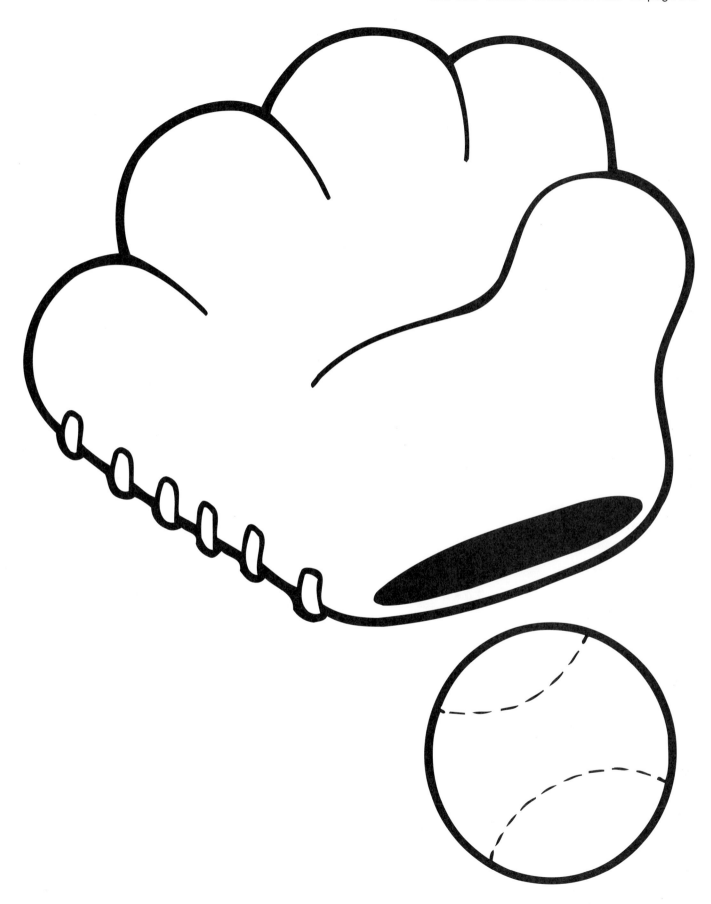

Patterns

Use with "It's Someone's Birthday!" on page 66.

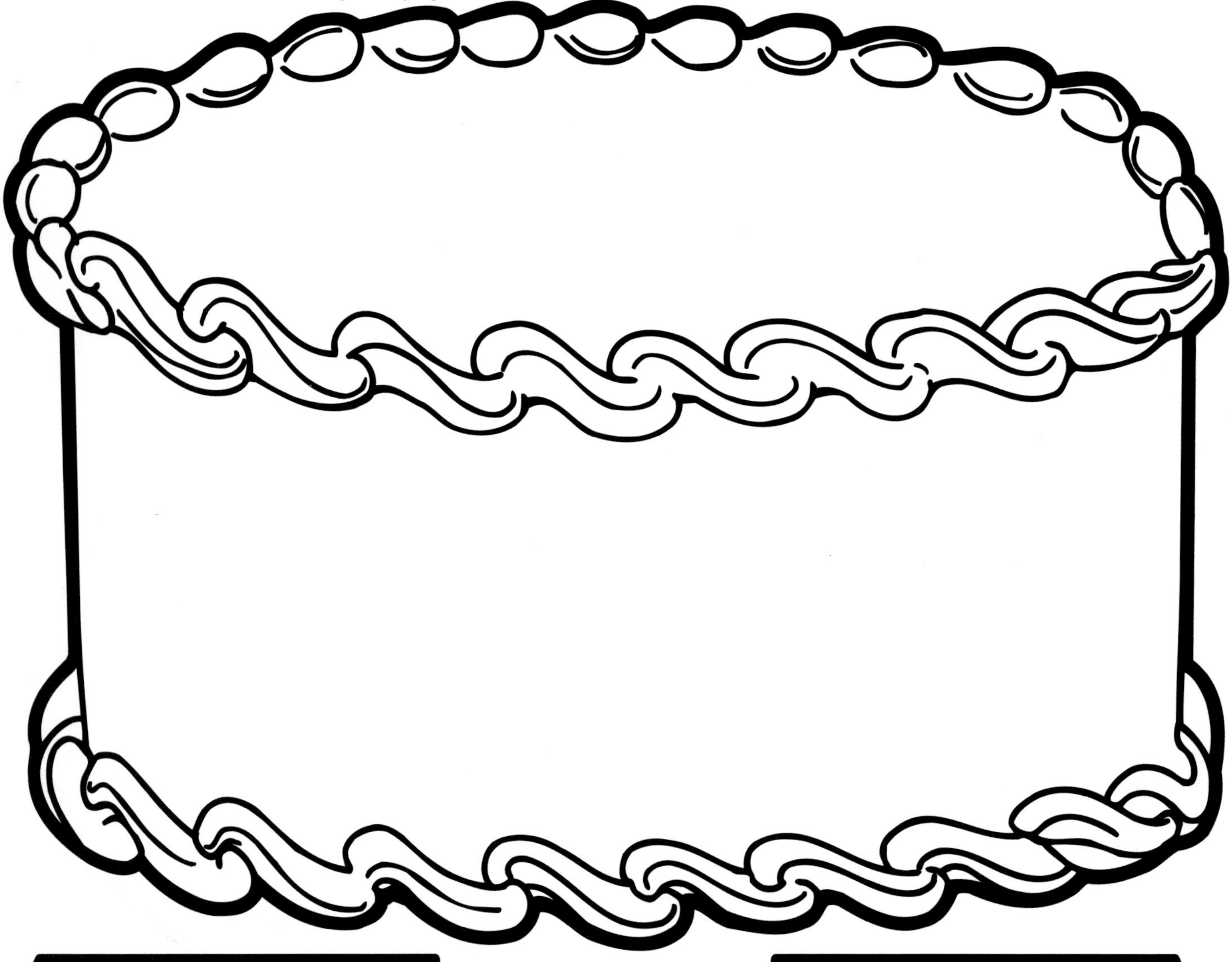

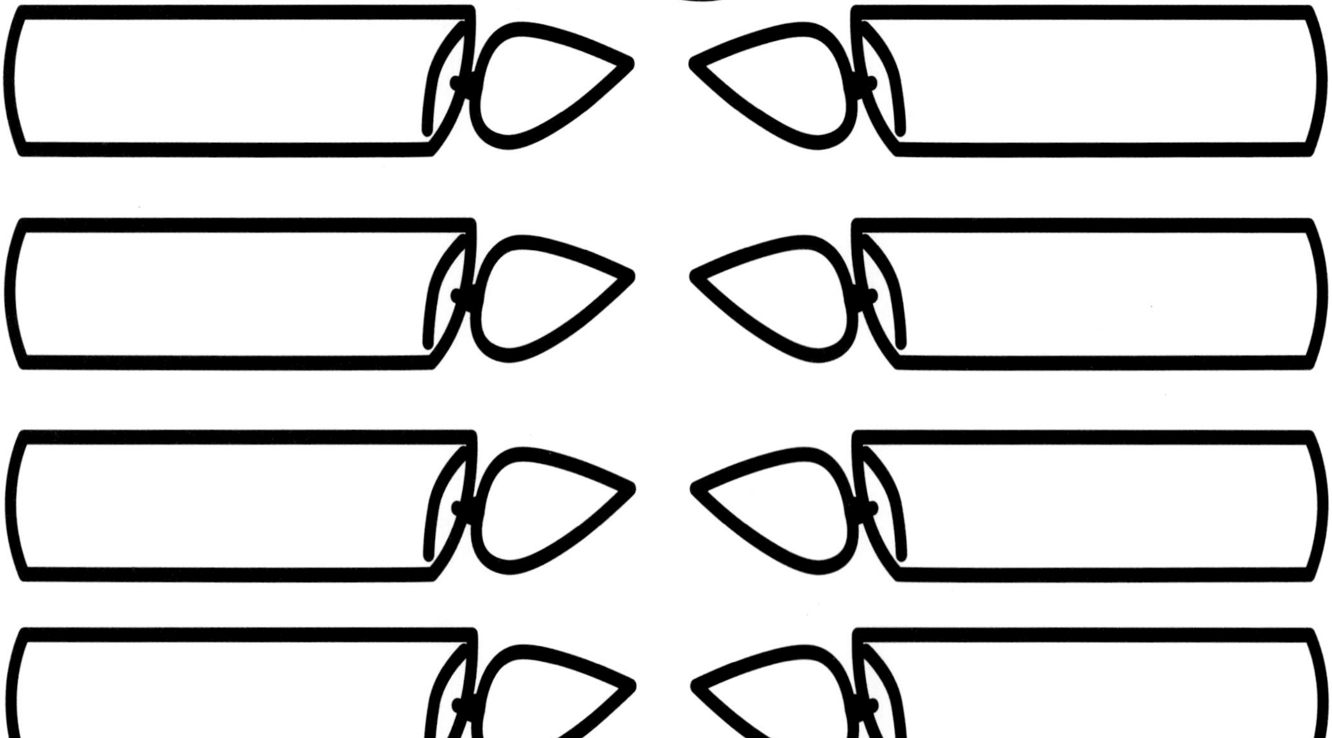

Patterns

Use with "This Year Will Be A Real Picnic" on page 67.